Other Titles by Pablo Helguera

Endingness: Prolegomena for a New Art of Memory

The Pablo Helguera Manual of Contemporary Art Style

The Witches of Tepoztlán (and Other Unpublished Operas)

The Boy Inside the Letter

Artoons (I, II & III)

The Juvenal Players

Suite Panamericana

Estela y las Hojas

Theatrum Anatomicum (and Other Performance Lectures)

What in the World

The School of Panamerican Unrest: An Anthology of Documents (with Sara Demeuse)

Urÿonstelaii

Onda Corta

Education for Socially Engaged Art (A Materials and Techniques Handbook)

Art Scenes: The Social Scripts of the Art World

HELGUERA'S

ARtunes

Helguera's

ArTunes

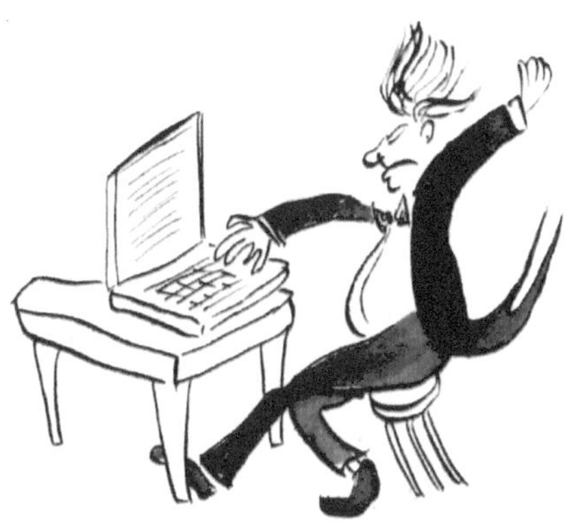

Classical Music Cartoons

By Pablo Helguera

Jorge Pinto Books Inc.
New York

ArTunes
By Pablo Helguera

Published by Jorge Pinto Books Inc., website: www.pintobooks.com

Book design by Charles King, website: www.ckmm.com

ISBN: 978-1-934978-77-1
ISBN-10: 1-934978-77-9

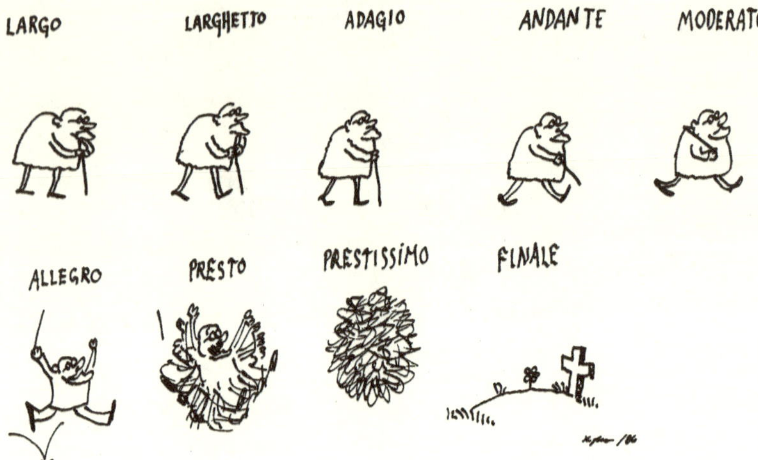
LARGO
LARGHETTO
ADAGIO
ANDANTE
MODERATO
ALLEGRO
PRESTO
PRESTISSIMO
FINALE

Foreword

If there's one thing the beleaguered classical music world could use right now — aside from an influx of listeners and cash — is way to laugh at itself.

We've been conditioned to believe that classical music is serious business for serious people. *Make sure to dress appropriately for the concert hall. Remember to refrain from applauding between movements. And for heaven's sake, do NOT crinkle candy wrappers in the middle of a Mahler symphony!* These are the kinds of rules that have shored up the fortress. To this day you can still find a kind of Ten Commandments of concert etiquette tucked inside program books at Washington D.C.'s Kennedy Center for the Performing Arts. Commandment number seven states: "Thou shalt not talk or hum, or sing along, or beat time with a body part." For me, it's all uncomfortably close to sitting in church.

And yet we wonder why orchestras and opera houses have trouble filling seats. Young people might rightly view the classical music experience as an opportunity to wear uncomfortable clothes, sit quiet and let the boredom begin — all the while missing out on texting, tweeting and a variety of other contemporary stimuli.

And then there are the persistent socio-political arguments: Classical music is the elitist art form of stuffy (and dead) European white guys playing to dwindling audiences of the rich and gray-haired. It's not really the fault of the music, it's the music's self-appointed guardians. But these problematic perceptions, as it turns out, are relatively recent.

Read Mozart's letters and you'll find that concertgoers in his day weren't so reverential. Writing from Paris in 1773, he describes an audience "sent into raptures," interrupting the first movement of his Symphony in D Major, applauding wildly and shouting for an encore. And 50 years before that, in Handel's day, operagoers routinely ate, drank and played cards during productions, quieting down only to catch the big arias. We wouldn't dream of such breaches of decorum today.

As for stereotyped composers — like solitary saints equipped with only their thoughts and fountain pens — it shouldn't come as a surprise that they were actually human. They reveled in their vices and virtues like anyone else. J.S. Bach, the man who gave us the sublime *St. Matthew Passion* was once tossed in jail for essentially telling his boss to take this job and shove it. Haydn placed practical jokes and folk tunes in his music. Even the gruff Beethoven who, when provoked, tended to throw either food or a lawsuit at his adversaries, wrote an irreverent little song called "Ass of All Asses."

Still, over the past century or so, barriers were built little by little, walling off classical music from popular culture. Thanks in part to finicky conductors, audiences were gradually cautioned to hush up and worship. And long gone it seems are the days when classical musicians appeared regularly on television and graced the covers of popular magazines.

So goodness knows, with a reputation of taking itself too seriously, classical music, with its recent spate of financial blunders and bitter labor disputes, could use a shot in the arm.

Here, with syringe at the ready, is Pablo Helguera. His prescription is humor and his medicine is the deceptively old-fashioned cartoon — or "artune" as he prefers.

Classical music comes naturally to Helguera. His father and uncles formed one of Mexico's only string quartets in the 1940s, his two sisters are professional musicians and his brother edited a prominent classical music magazine. Although claiming to be no composer, Helguera's piece *Endingness* — part of a larger work that also included a sculpture of framed beeswax and an essay — was performed by the Detroit Symphony Orchestra in 2011.

As a kid, Helguera dreamed of being an opera singer, but didn't go much beyond memorizing vast swaths of Puccini and belting it out in the shower. He gradually became the family's visual artist. He recently sent me an amusing batch of cartoons he drew as a 15-year-old growing up in Mexico City (see page *viii*). Already, his keen perspective and sharp wit are abundantly clear.

Although Helguera eventually landed in New York

as a serious artist, trafficking in topics from pedagogy and sociolinguistics to ethnography and *Education for Socially Engaged Art* (a book he wrote last year), his love music and humor never left him.

"I had stopped making cartoons publicly — only for friends and family — for many years," Helguera told me recently. "But with the advent of social media, making cartoons felt like a good way to communicate again; it felt right." He started drawing *New Yorker*-style cartoons for art publications, "They were my therapy," he says. And later he collected them in the 2009 book *Artoons*.

A year later, as I was launching *Deceptive Cadence*, NPR Music's classical music blog, a chance meeting with a colleague of mine brought Helguera and me together. What about a classical music cartoon, published every Friday at noon? It seemed like an idea worth trying at the time. Now, two years down the road, it still seems fresh to me. No one else regularly comments on the state of the art in this medium. It's from these Friday high noon musical missives that this book is derived.

Sometimes I think of Helguera as a court jester, holding up a mirror to those self-appointed guardians of classical music, sketching out in humor what we're sometimes afraid to verbalize, while exploding myths and sweeping away fusty traditions. The mirror extends to us, too. What we find in his art reflects our own relationship with this noble, mysteriously powerful and embattled music. I find that while Helguera's "artunes" elicit laughs, they also convince me of the continued resiliency of symphonies and operas, sonatas and songs — and the men and women who create and recreate them.

— Tom Huizenga, November, 2012

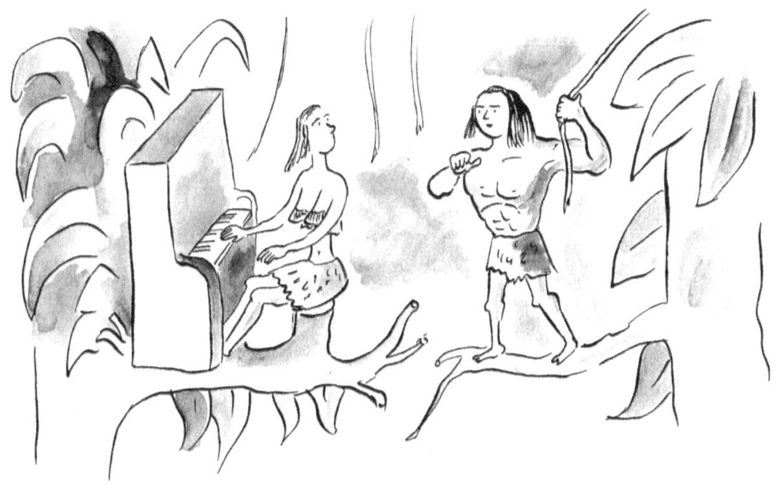

"Me, Robert; you, Clara."

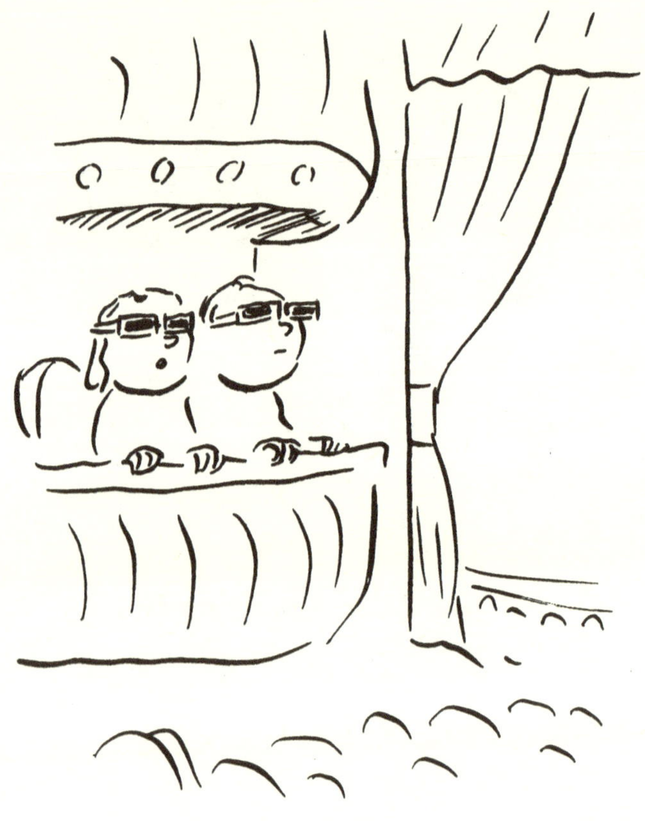

"The only problem with 3-D opera is that the tenor's ego looks even bigger."

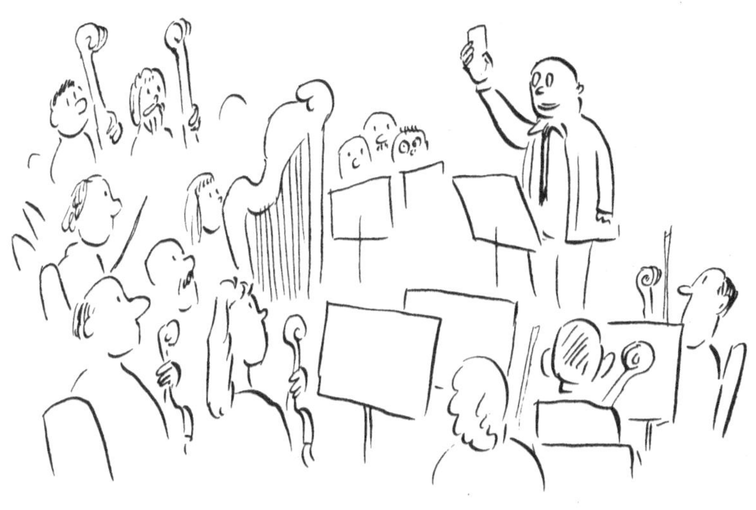

"After an extensive search for a new conductor, the board decided you guys will be better off being conducted by an app."

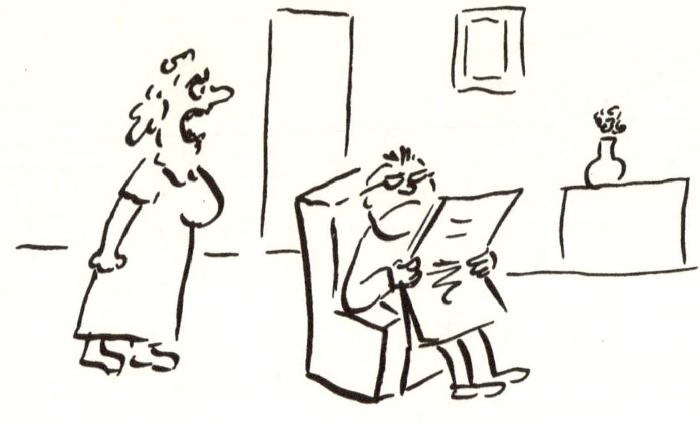

"And I haven't even begun to argue – that was just the recitativo!"

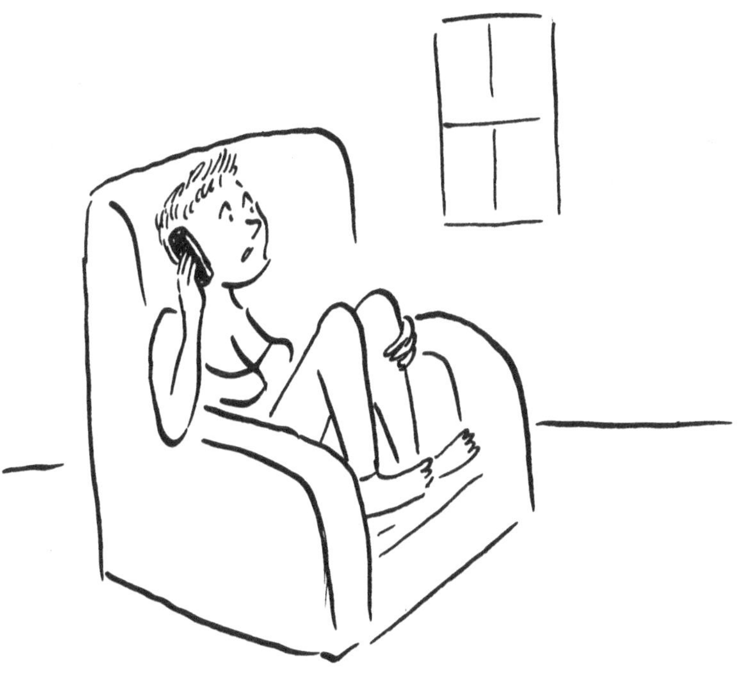

"Are you with another woman or are you speaking in falsetto to yourself?"

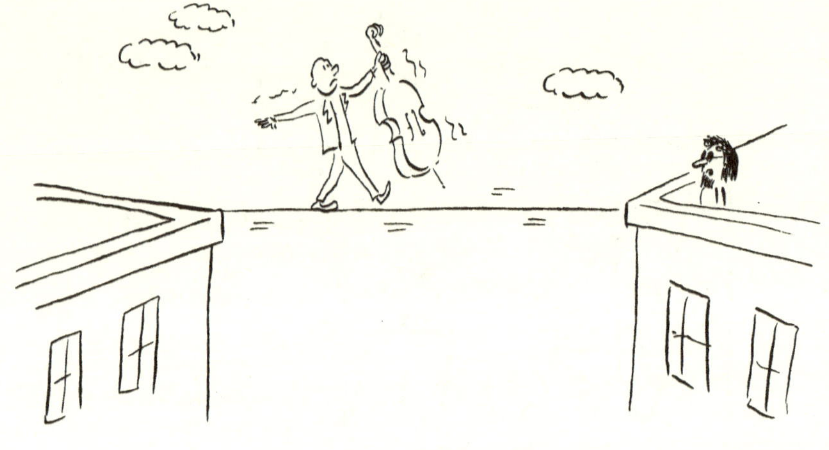

"Are you sure you want to cross over into Pop?"

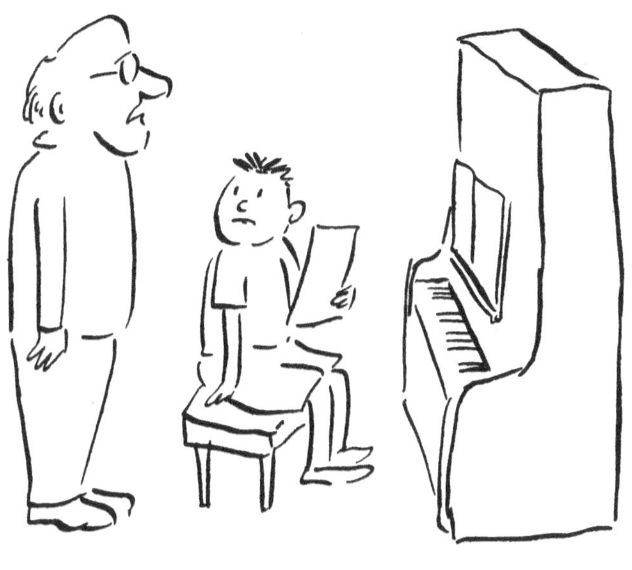

"Before I heard you play it, that used to be my favorite piece."

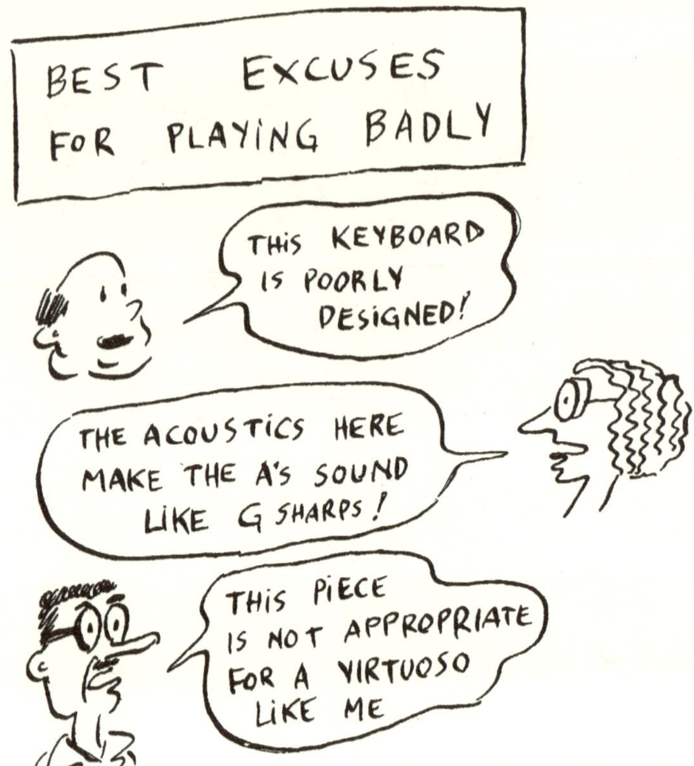
BEST EXCUSES FOR PLAYING BADLY
THIS KEYBOARD IS POORLY DESIGNED!
THE ACOUSTICS HERE MAKE THE A'S SOUND LIKE G SHARPS!
THIS PIECE IS NOT APPROPRIATE FOR A VIRTUOSO LIKE ME

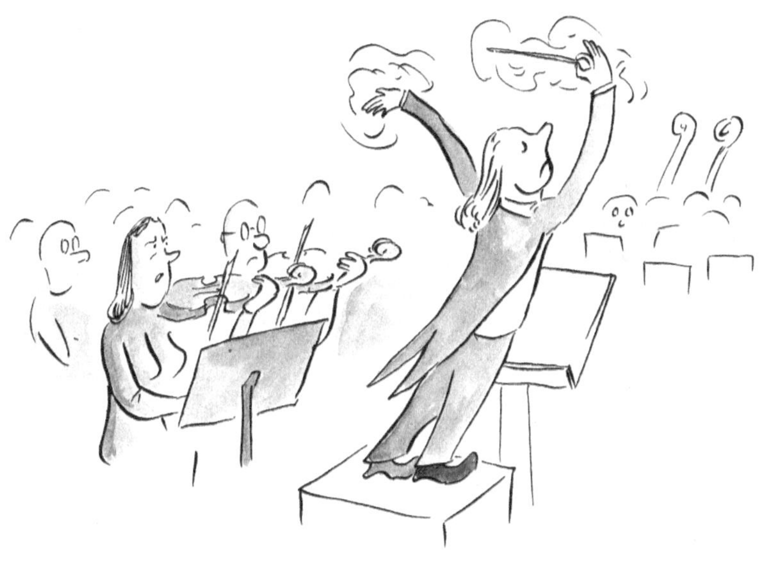

"I can't even follow him on Twitter."

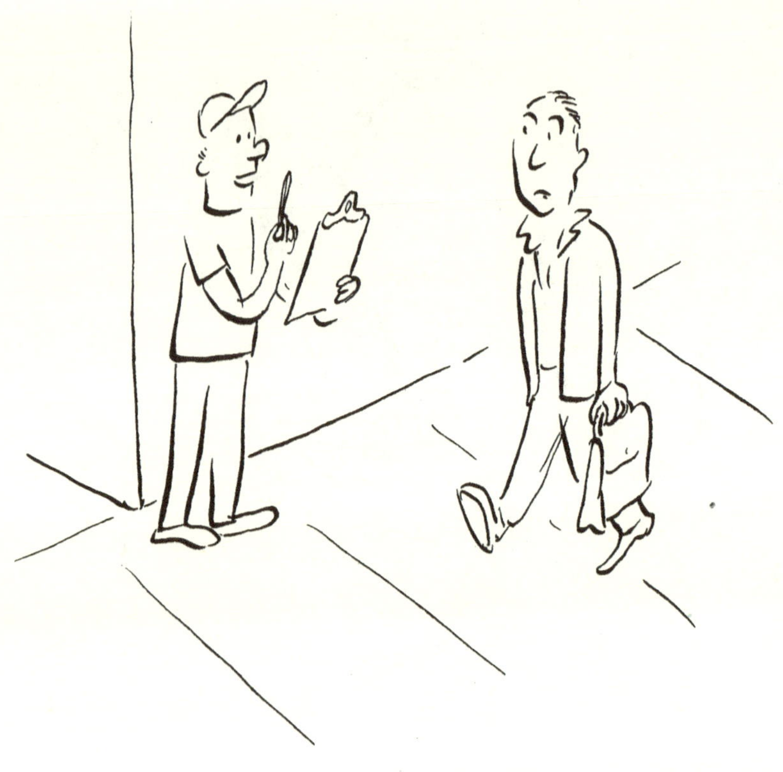

"Do you have a minute today to save the celesta player?"

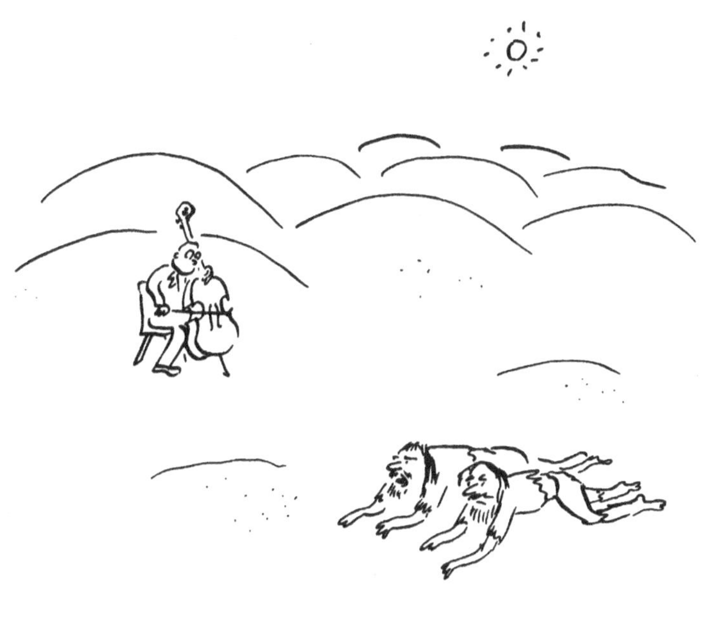

"I tell you we are going in circles – I swear I've seen this performance of the cello suites before."

CLASSICAL OLYMPICS

HANDEL AQUATICS

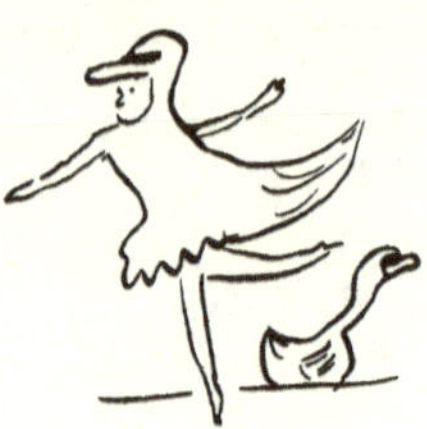

TCHAIKOVSKY FIGURE SKATING

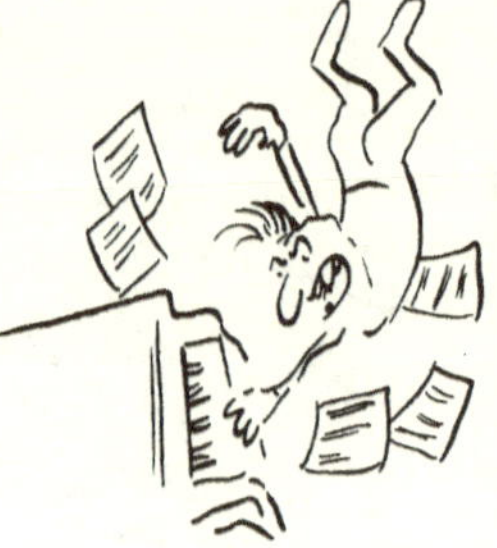

FREESTYLE WRESTLING WITH A LISZT SCORE

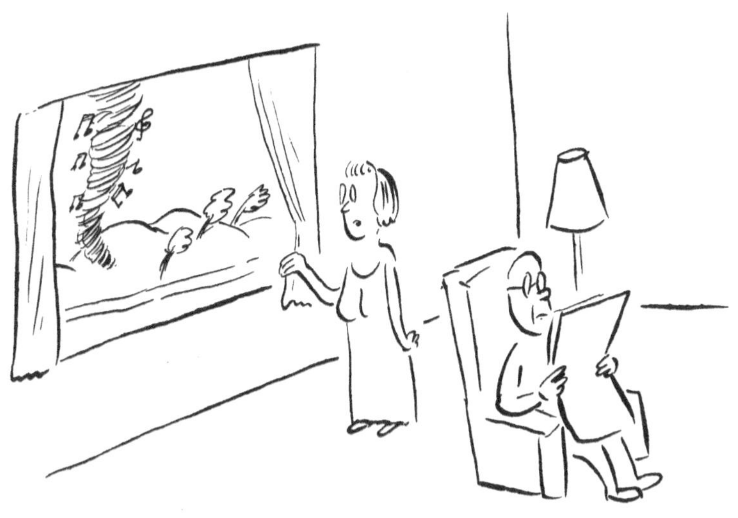

"Concert season is upon us."

DANCE OF THE HIGH-FRUCTOSE CORN SYRUP PLUM FAIRIES

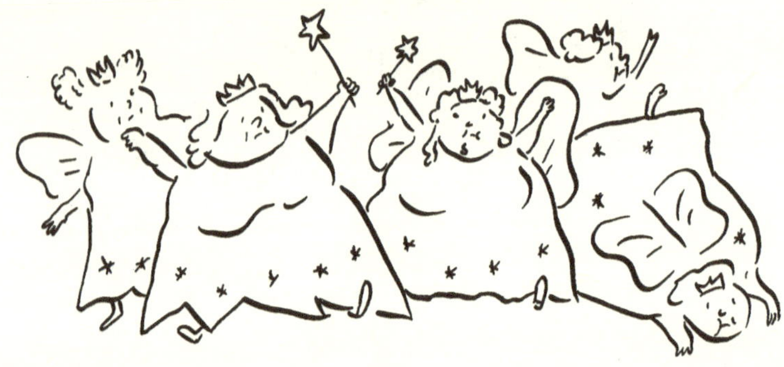

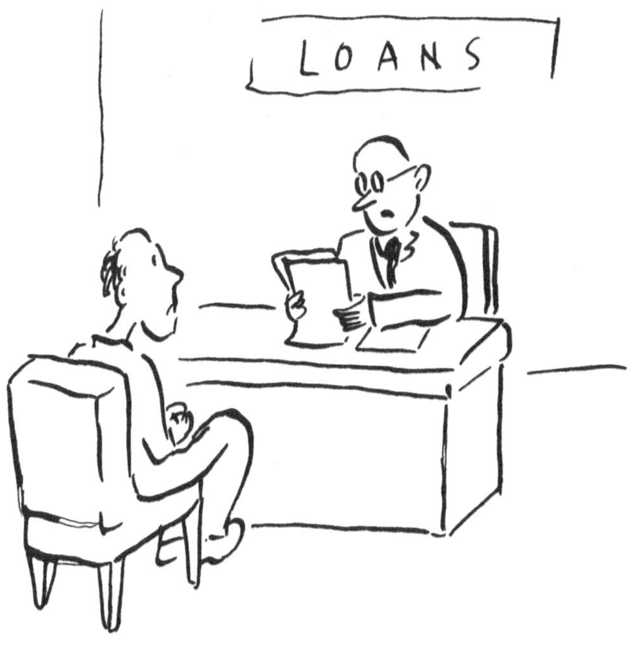

"Your debts are in crescendo, your savings in diminuendo, and your credit is dissonant."

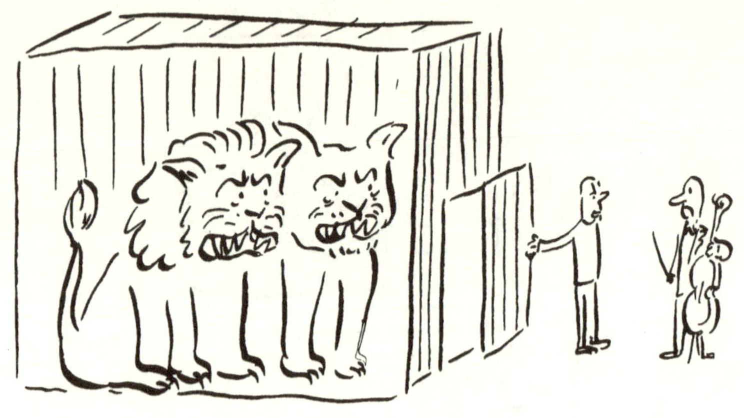

"Don't worry – it's just an audition."

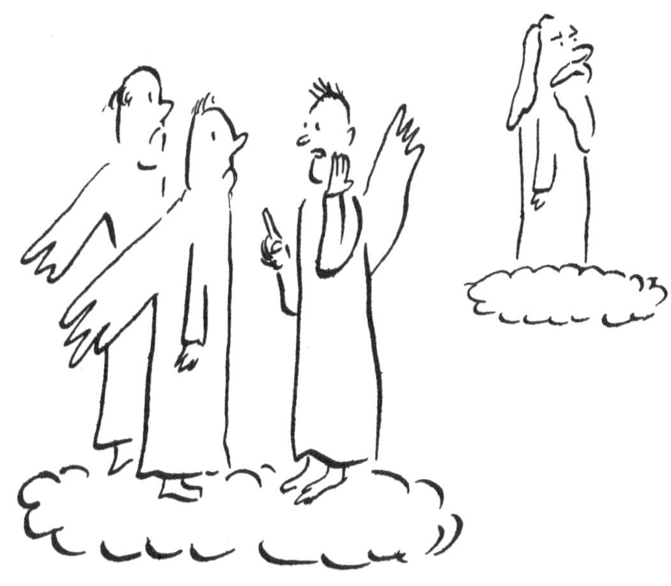

"Oh, yes, and one more thing . . . don't call him God Almighty. He prefers 'maestro.'"

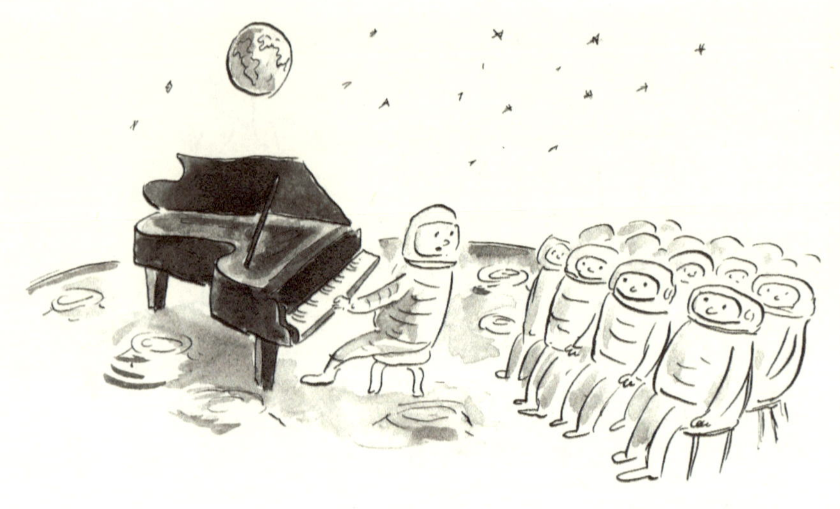

"And now, the immortal Earthlight Sonata."

EINSTEIN ON THE (HIGH SEASON) BEACH

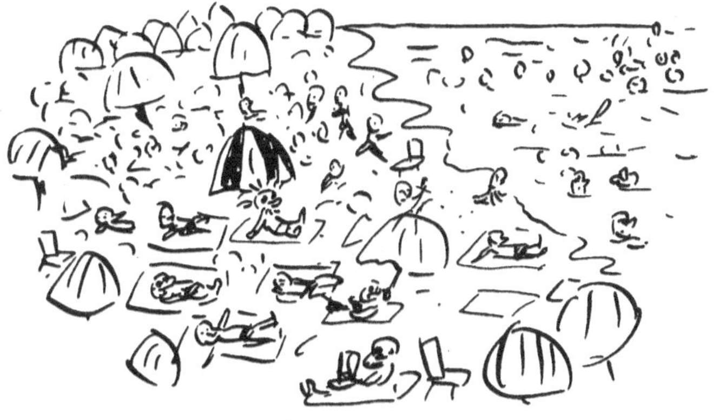

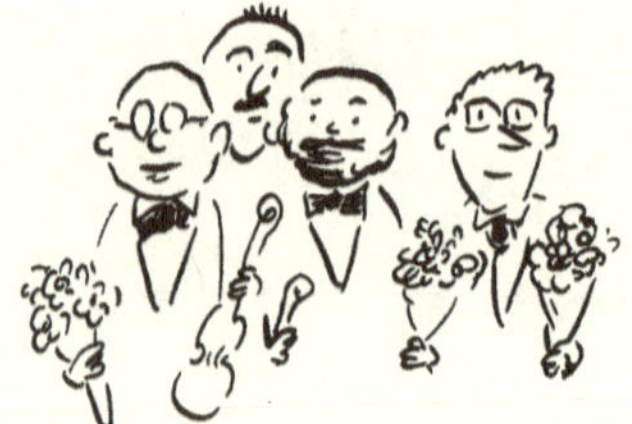

POTPOURRI QUARTET

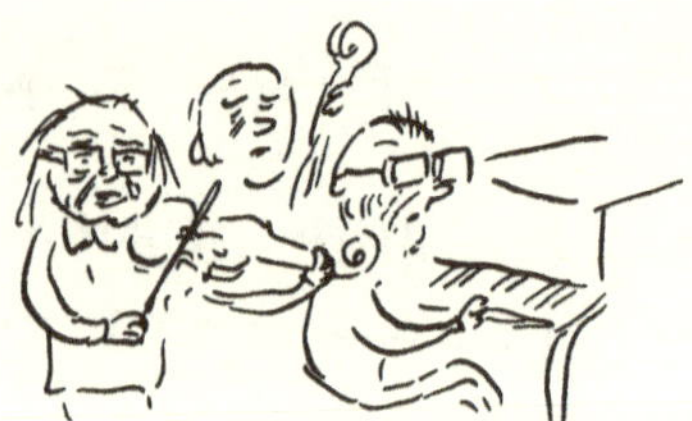

PASSÉ TRIO

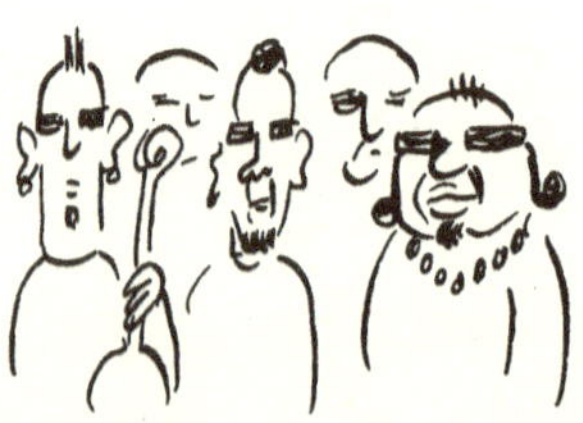

BUXTEHUDE - STOCKHAUSEN - MANCINI - BONO QUINTET

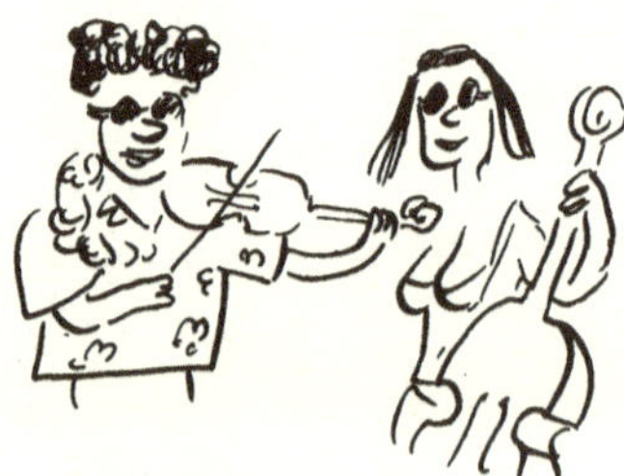

ALOHA BAROQUE ENSEMBLE

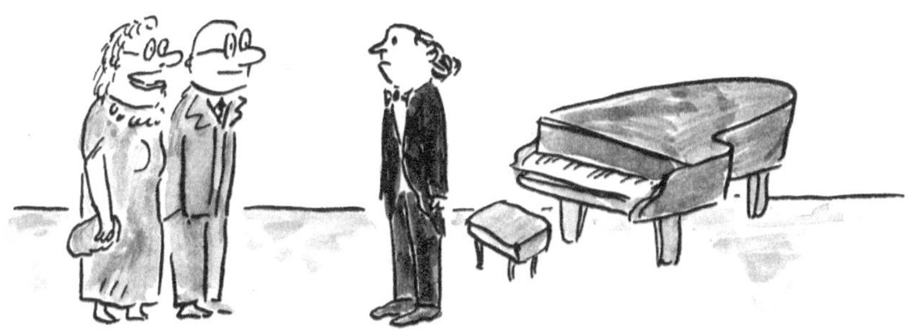

"Your playing was so-so, but your facial expressions were absolutely phenomenal!"

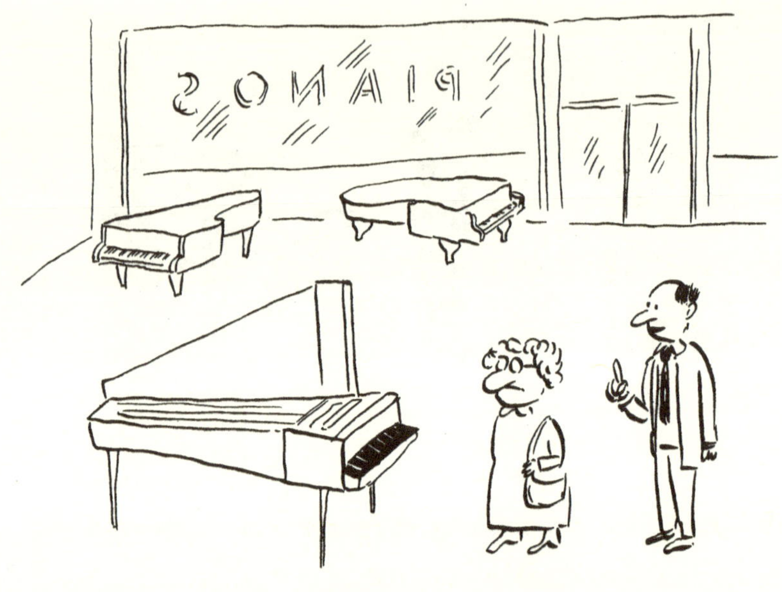

"And as part of our Black Friday promotion,
for every purchase of three harpsichords,
you get the fourth at 50% off."

YOUR NEIGHBORS' FREE NIGHT CONCERT

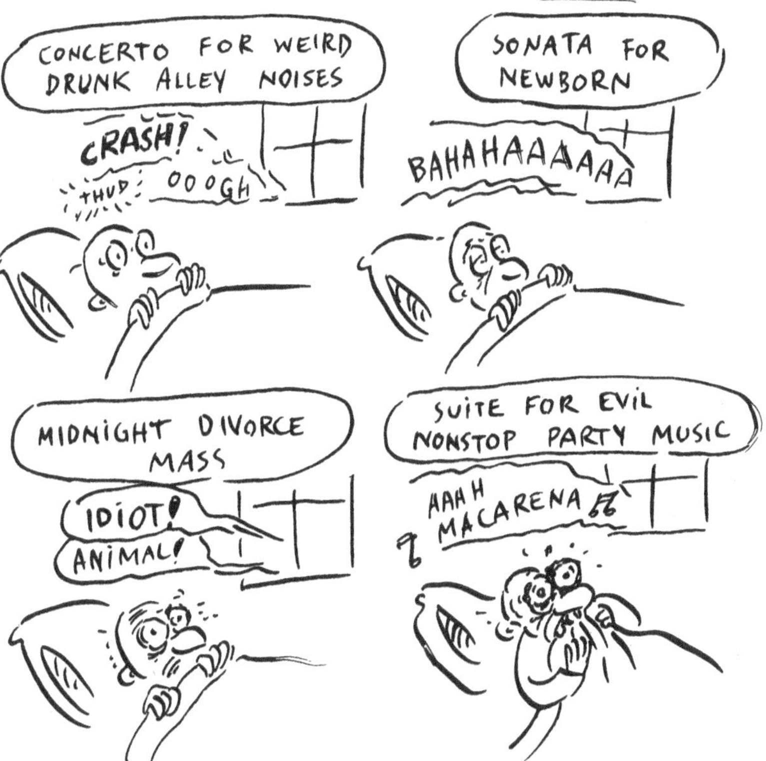

THE GOLDMAN SACHS VARIATIONS

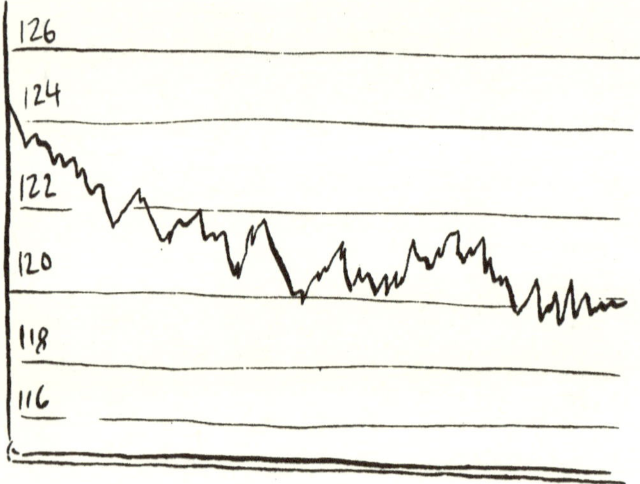

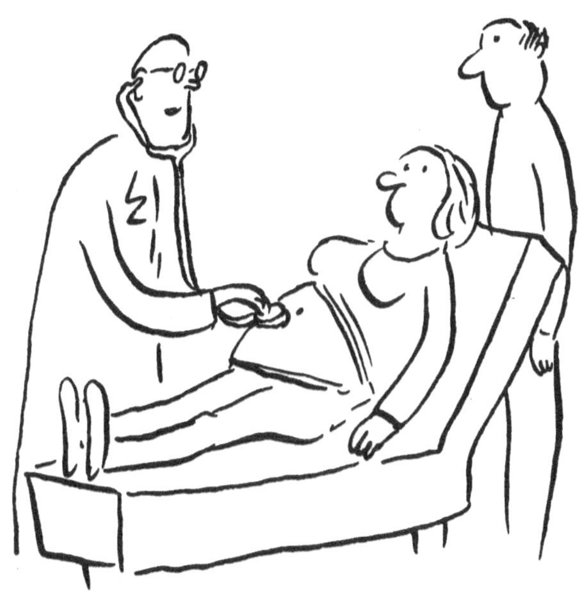

"He is developing nicely – he's playing Chopin's Mazurka in C Minor."

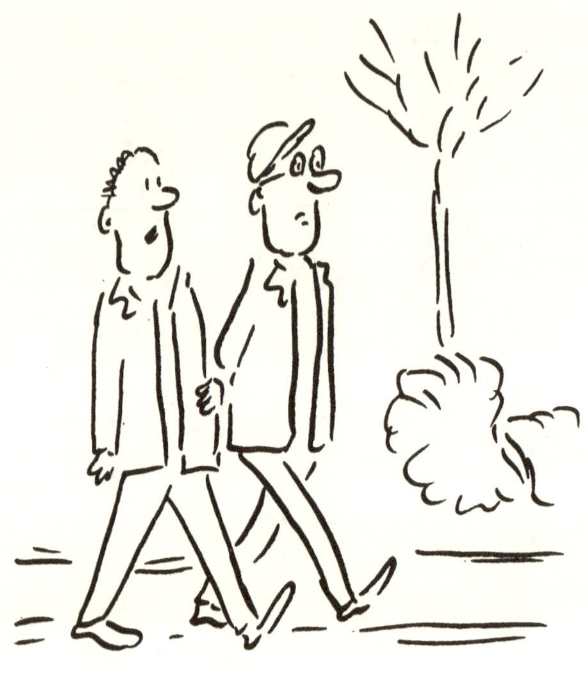

"I ate so much over the holidays that I went on a diet of light classics."

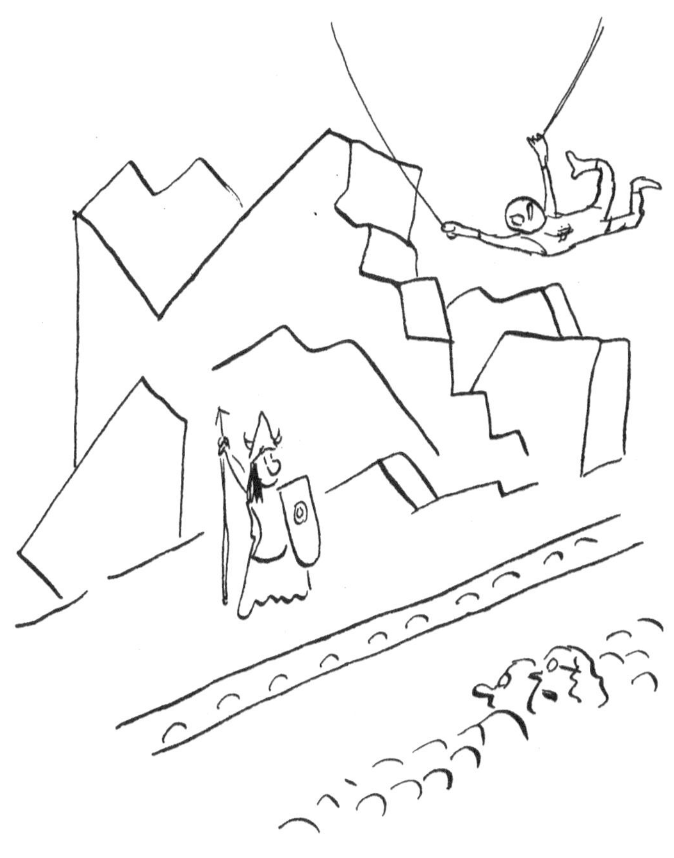

"I know it's a modern production of The Ring –
I'm just wondering about the inclusion of Spiderman."

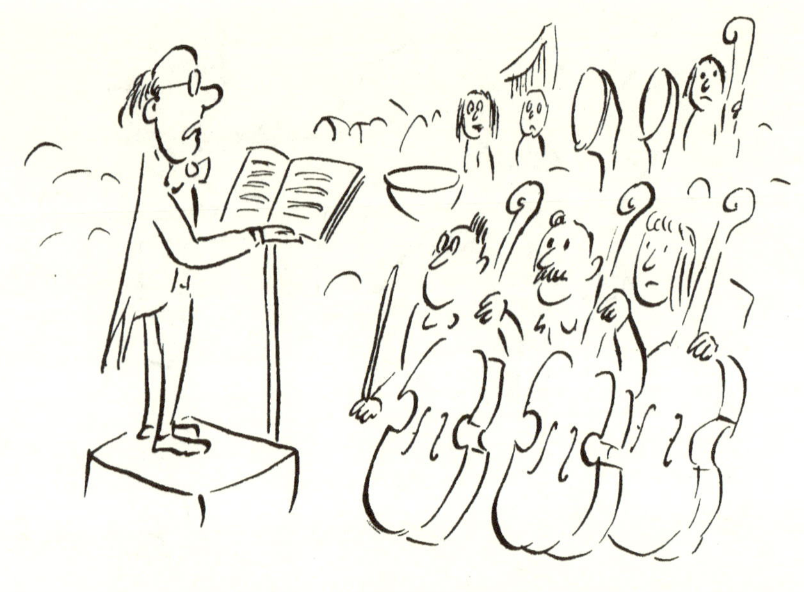

"I suggest we just lip-synch this whole movement."

IF OPERAS WERE BEERS

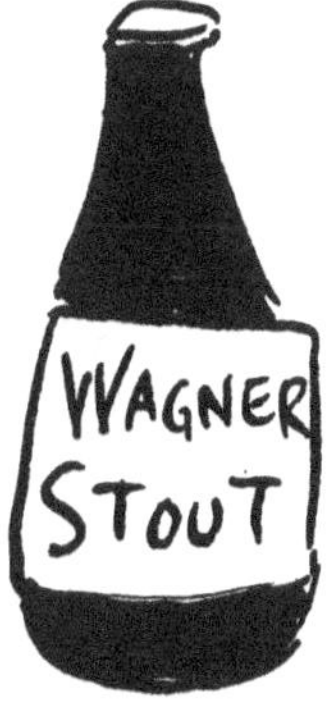

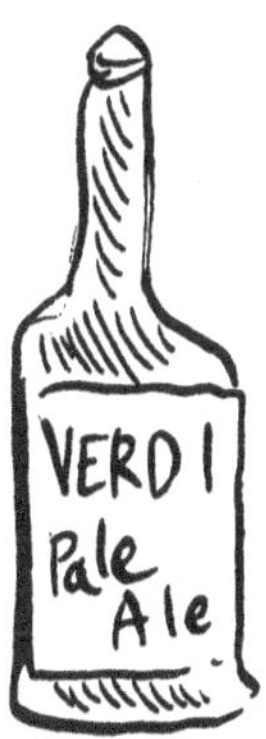

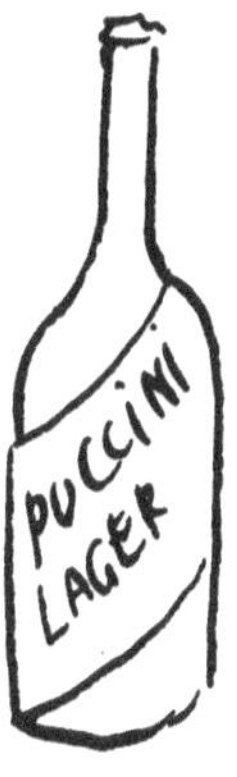

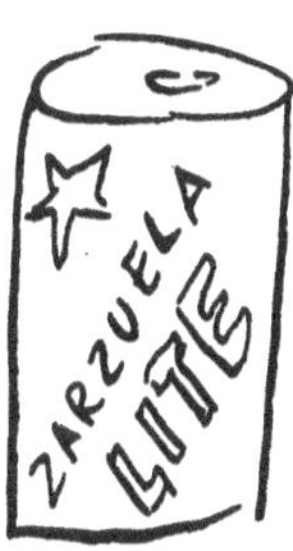

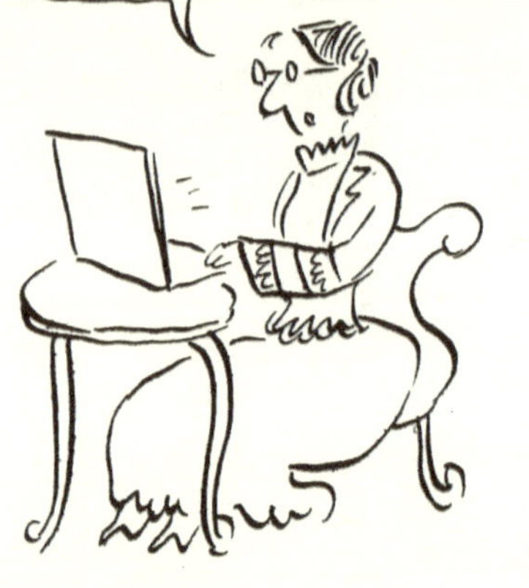
IF WAGNER HAD A BLOG
RICHARD DEAR, WHY CAN'T YOU WRITE SHORT POSTS LIKE EVERYONE ELSE?

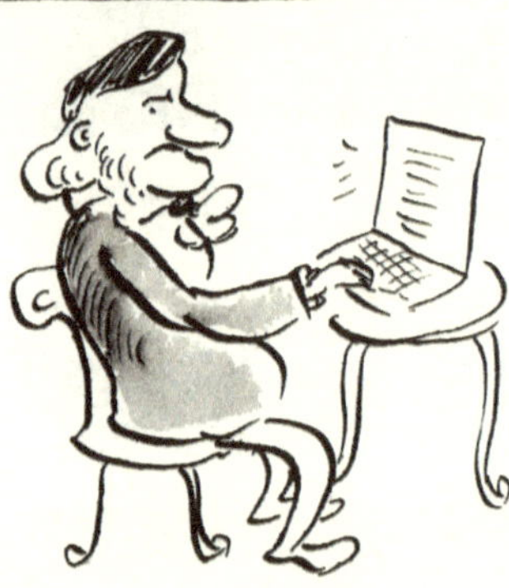

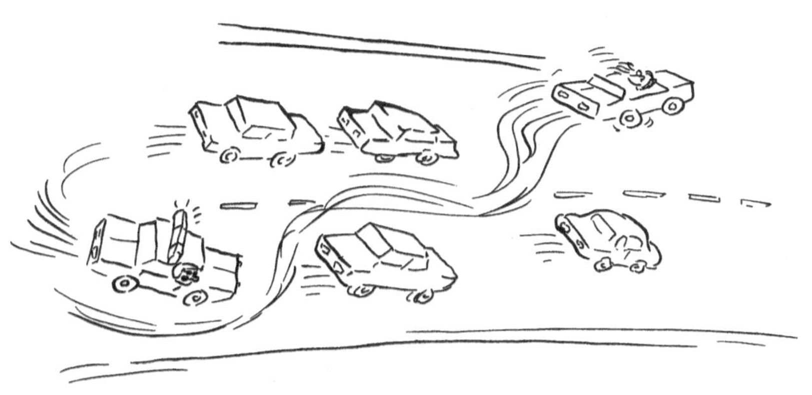

"He is impossible to follow – he must be an orchestra conductor."

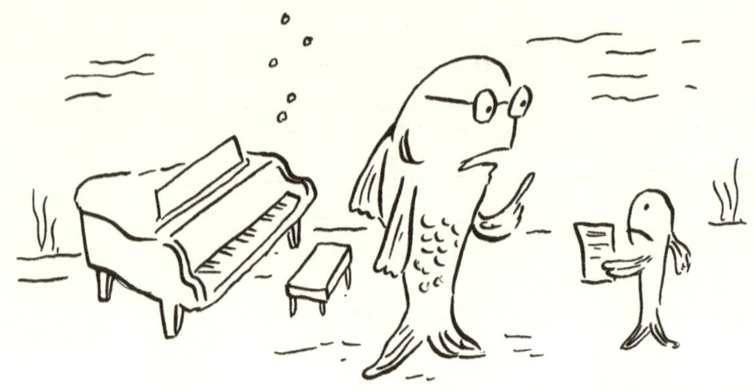

"Sorry, son – in order to play Liszt you would need to be an octopus."

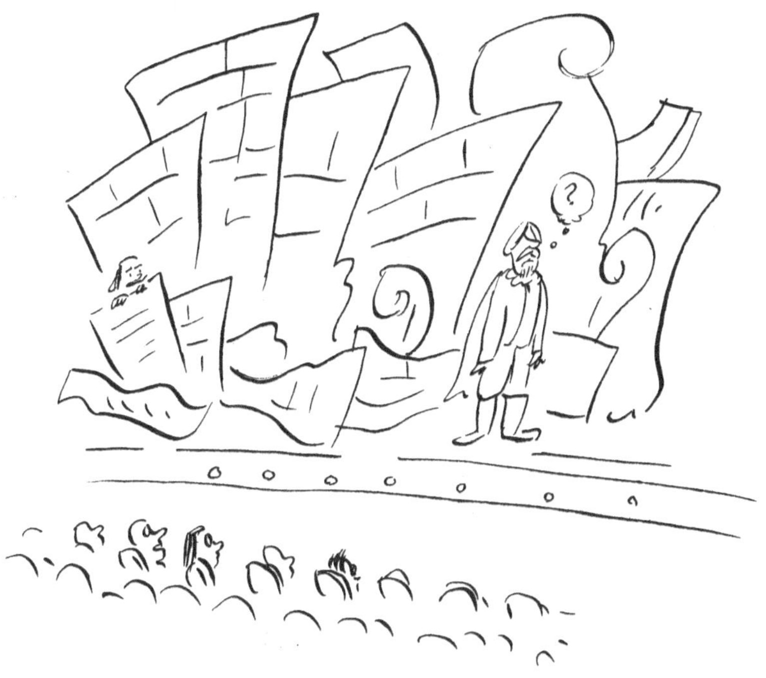

"In this act, the Commendatore can't take Don Giovanni to Hell because he gets lost in the set designed by Frank Gehry."

INSIGHTFUL COMMENTS FROM YOUR NON-CLASSICALLY INCLINED FRIENDS

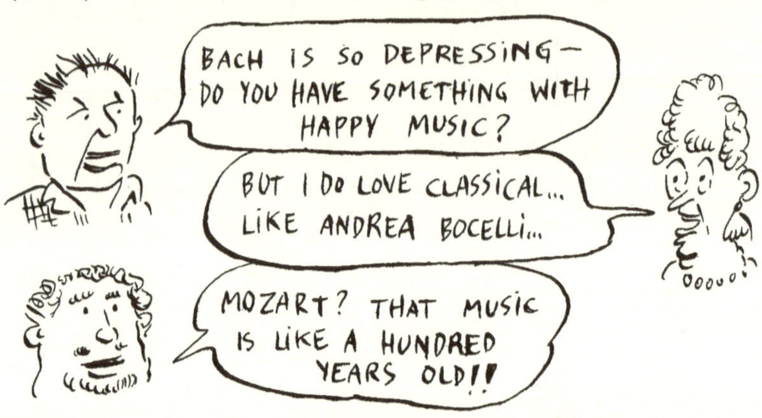

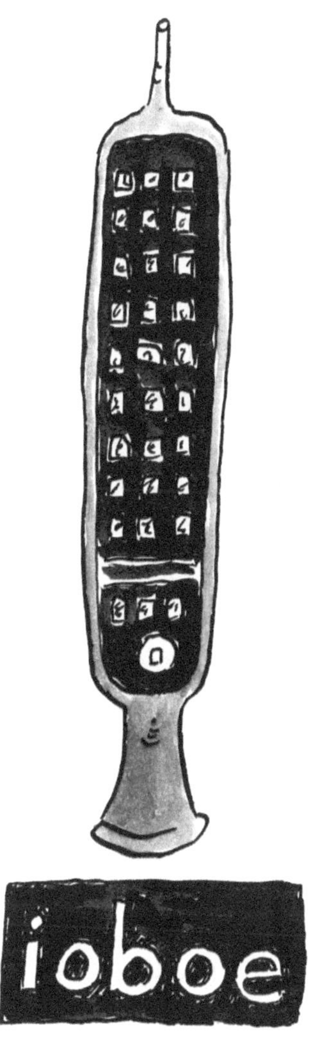
ioboe

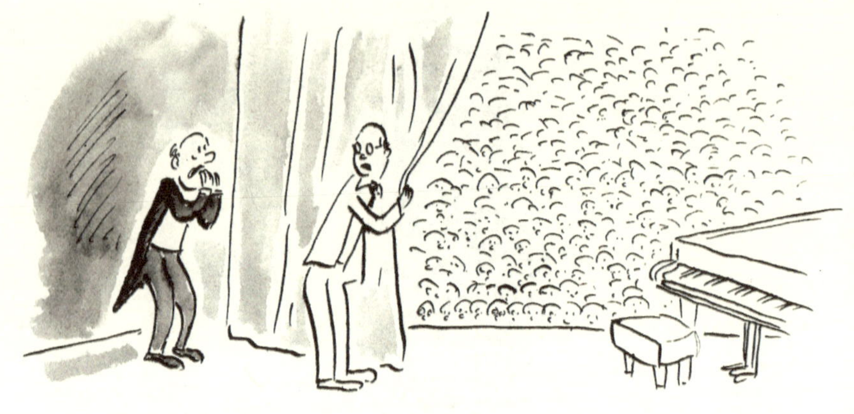

"It's just some of your Facebook fans."

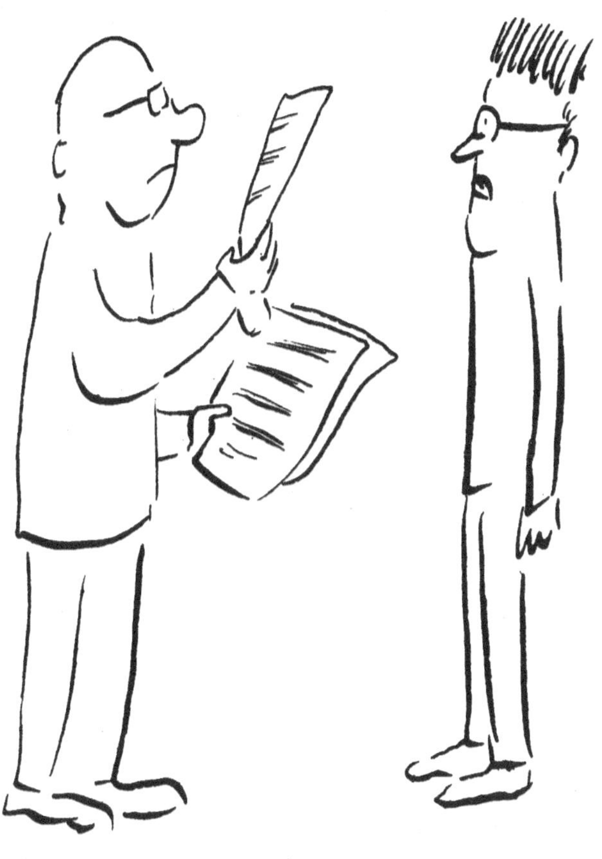

"It's not plagiarism – I am saving the planet by recycling the music of others."

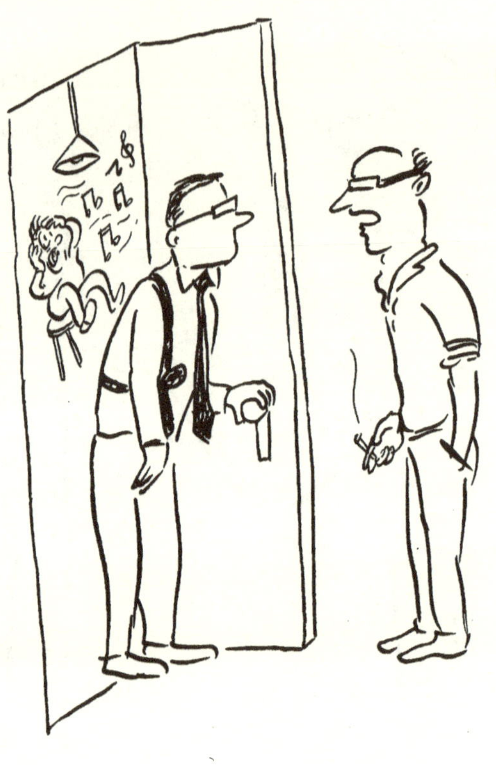

"Just keep playing the Bolero until he confesses."

L'APRÈS-MIDI D'UN FAUNE DANS SON CUBICLE

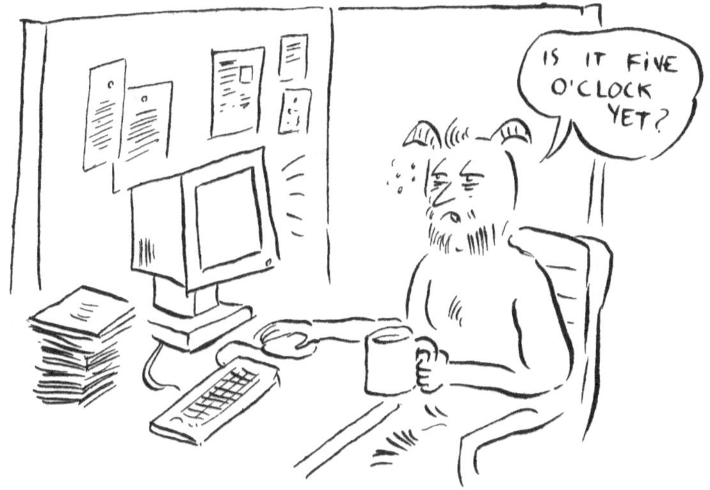

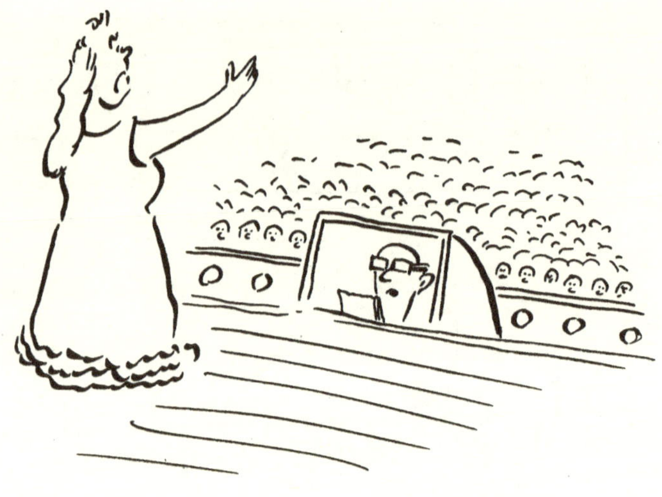

"OK – let's start by correcting your inflated bio in the program notes."

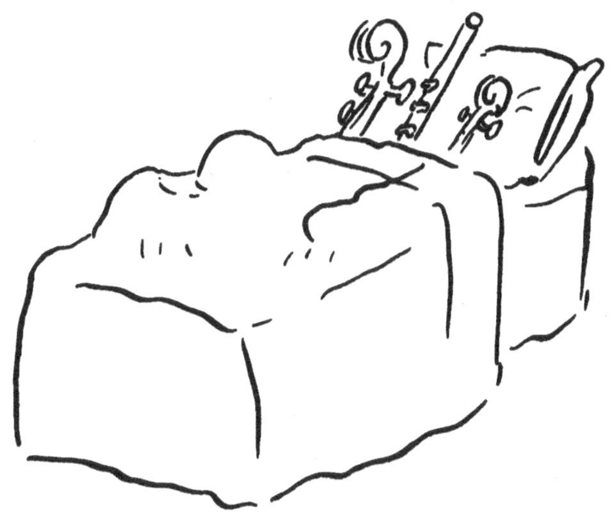

MÉNAGE À TRIO

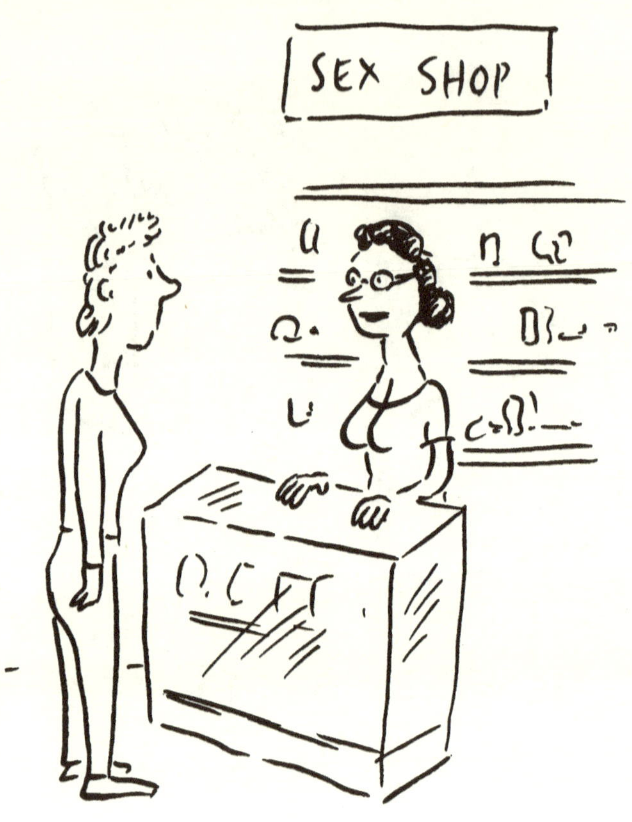

"Are you looking for glissando or vibrato products?"

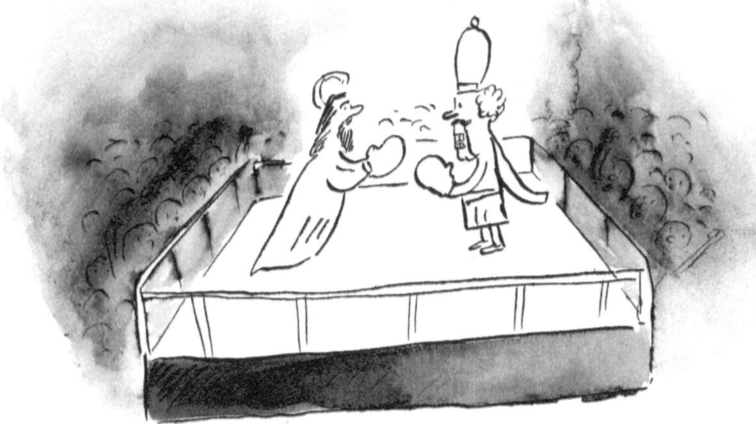
MESSIAH VS. NUTCRACKER

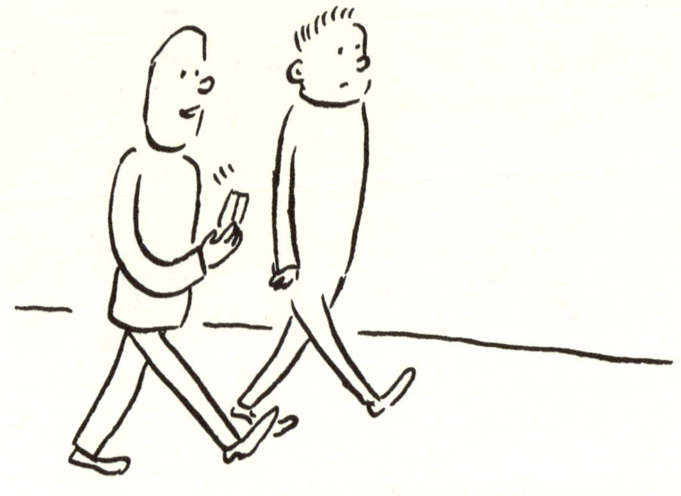

"I've just got Mozart's latest tweet – Köchel #87638."

NEW CLASSICAL MUSIC SUMMER FESTIVALS

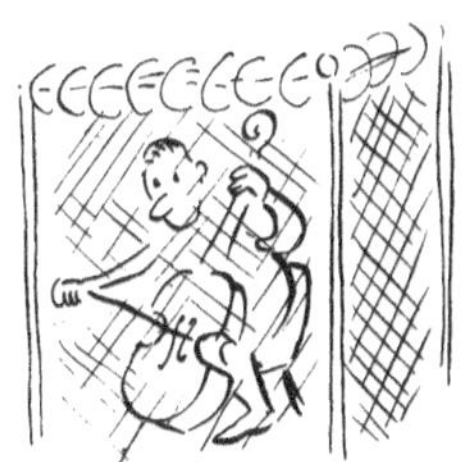

MOSTLY MOZART IN ALCATRAZ

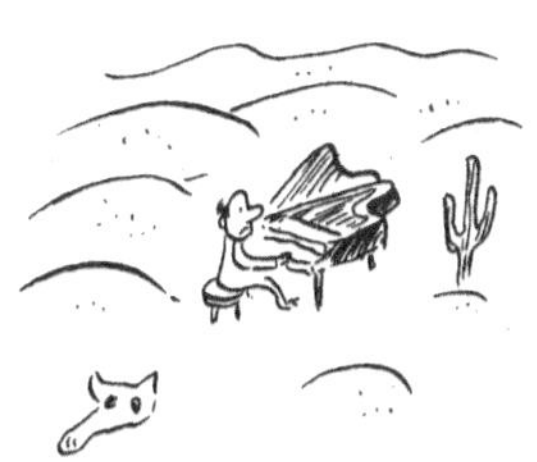

SCHUBERT IN DEATH VALLEY FEST

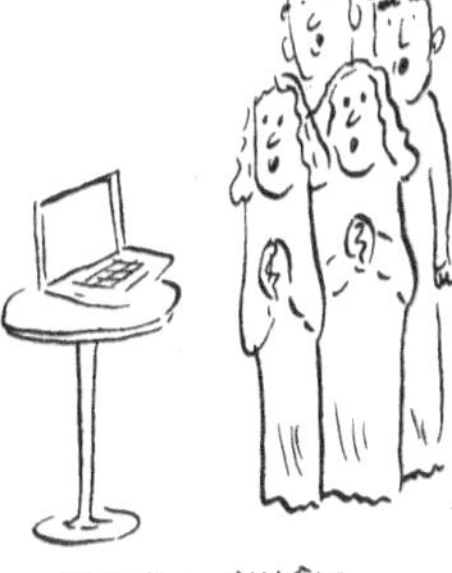

EARLY MUSIC SKYPE FEST

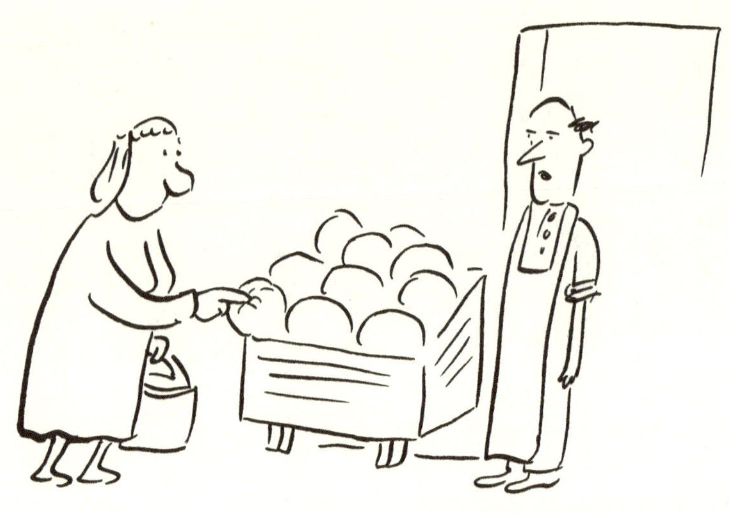

"No pizzicato, please."

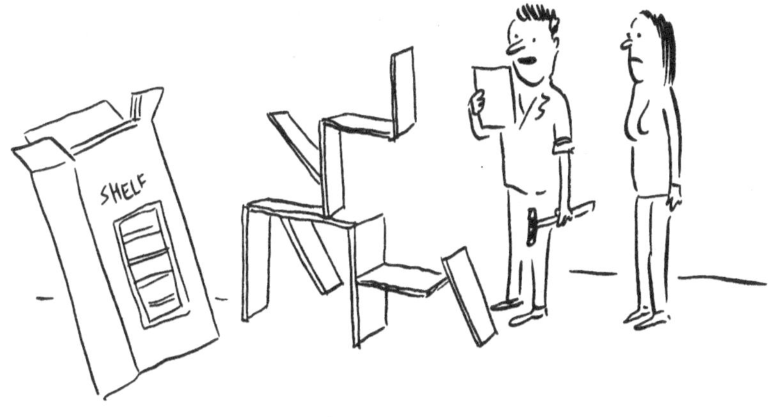

"Now I see the problem – I was reading the instructions like a John Cage score."

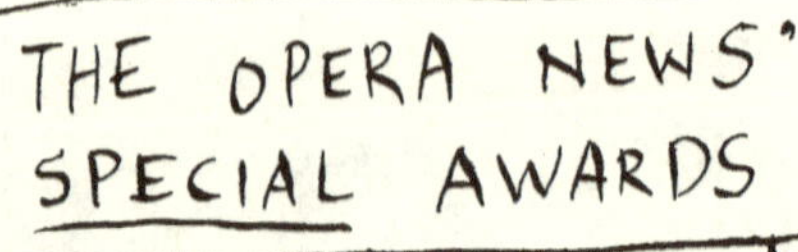

LEAST BANKRUPT ORCHESTRA

MOST UNPRONOUNCEABLE FOREIGN SINGER NAME

YEVGENIYJ ZHÖJRTQFYWÖTJK

MOST UNWANTED ENCORES

WE'LL REPEAT THE WHOLE THIRD ACT!

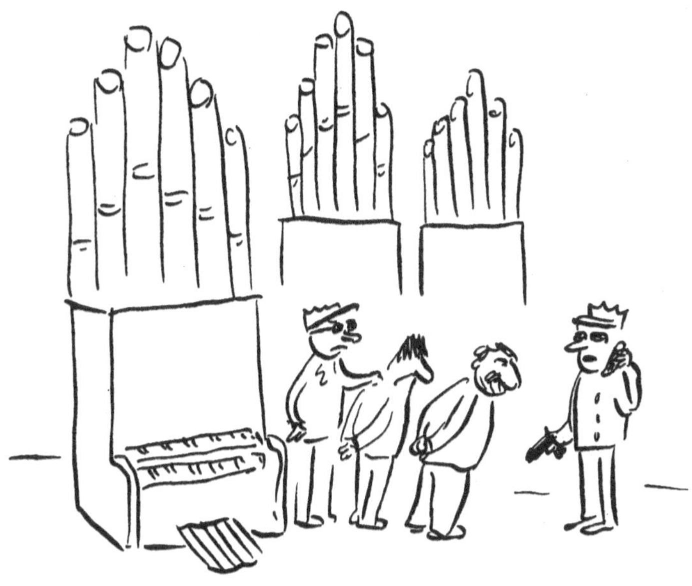

"We uncovered an organ trafficking operation."

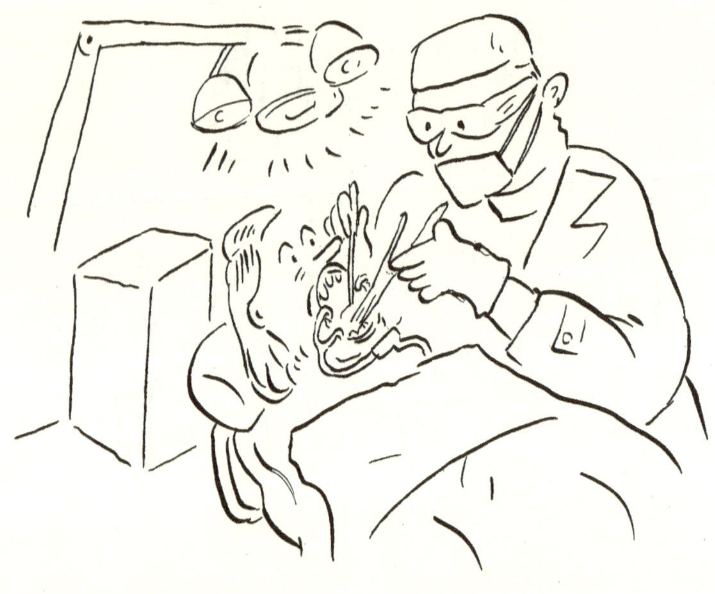

"OK, and now I will ask you to firmly hold your tongue on the roof of your mouth and accurately whistle La Polonaise."

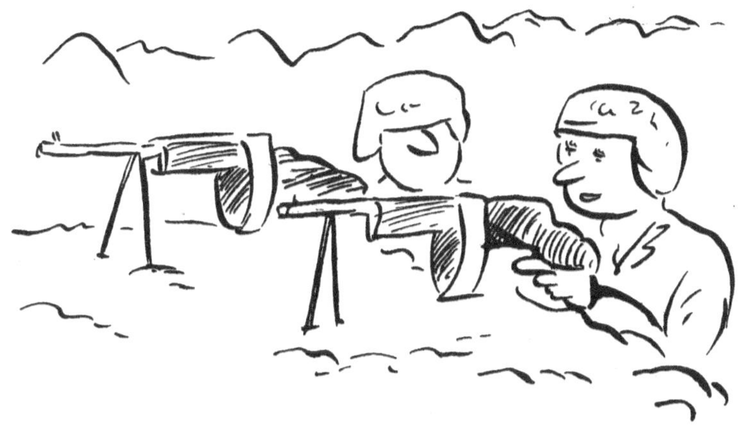

"All I wanted to be was a Puccini heroine."

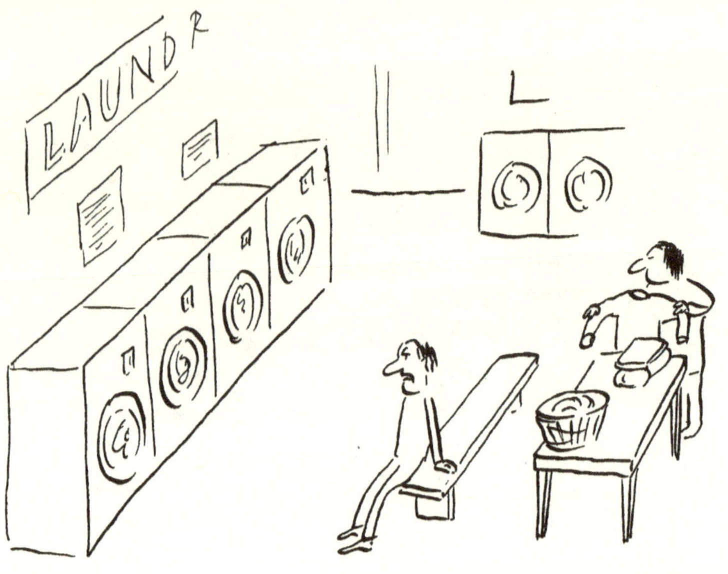

"This is taking forever – I shouldn't have put the load on the Ring cycle."

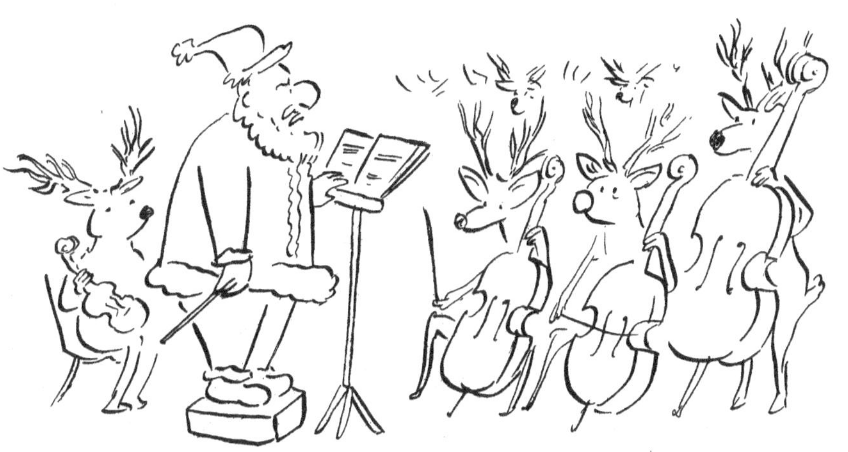

"Rudolf! Your nose keeps shining on the wrong measure!"

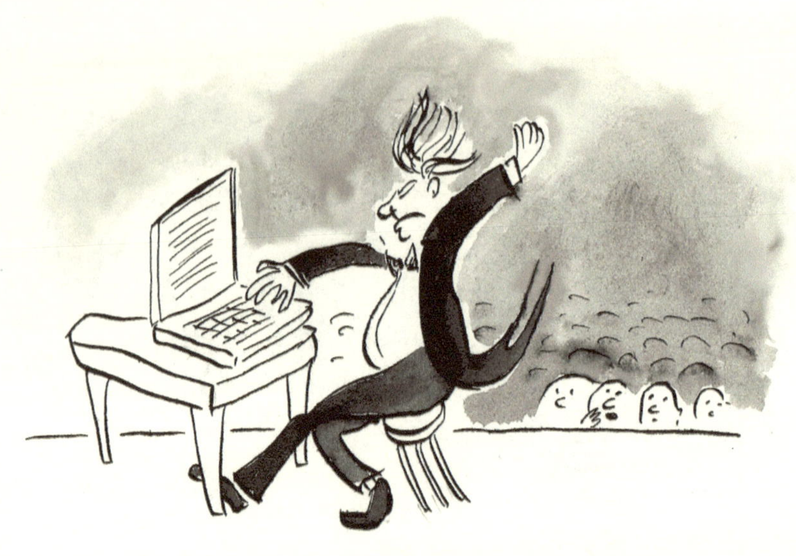

"He has a Russian blogging technique."

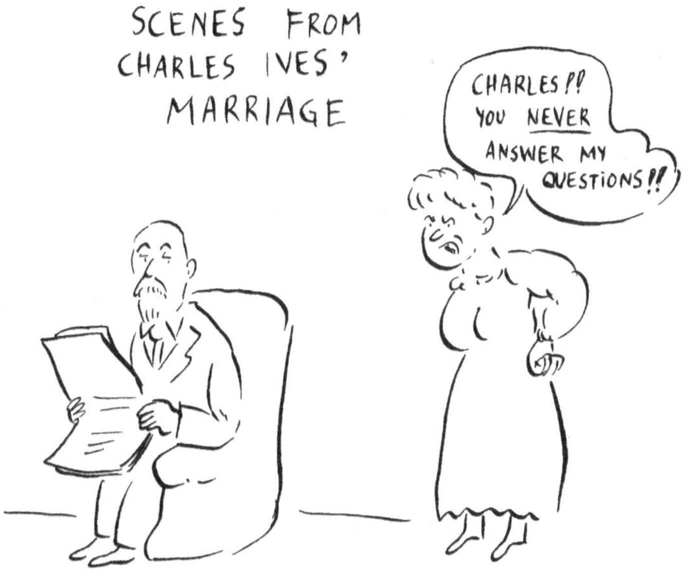
SCENES FROM
CHARLES IVES'
MARRIAGE
CHARLES?!
YOU NEVER
ANSWER MY
QUESTIONS!!

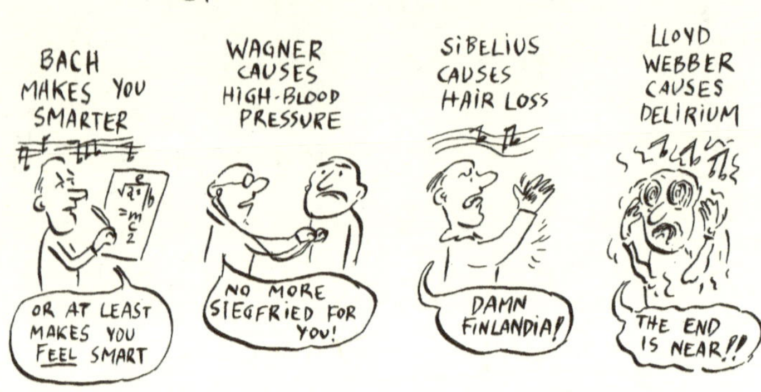
SCIENTIFICALLY PROVEN EFFECTS OF SOME COMPOSERS
BACH MAKES YOU SMARTER
OR AT LEAST MAKES YOU FEEL SMART
WAGNER CAUSES HIGH-BLOOD PRESSURE
NO MORE SIEGFRIED FOR YOU!
SIBELIUS CAUSES HAIR LOSS
DAMN FINLANDIA!
LLOYD WEBBER CAUSES DELIRIUM
THE END IS NEAR!!

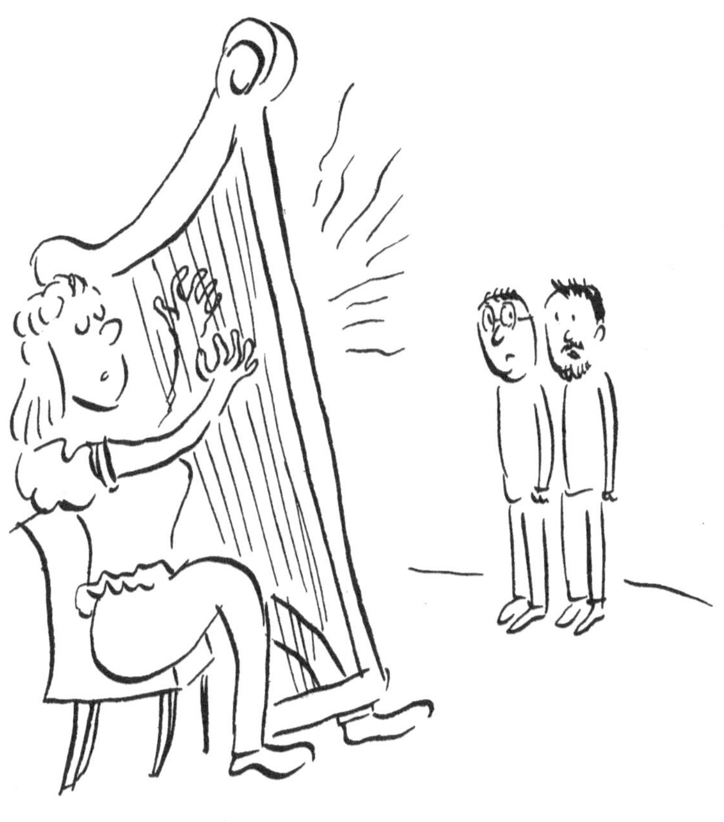

"She spends half her life tuning and the other half playing out of tune"

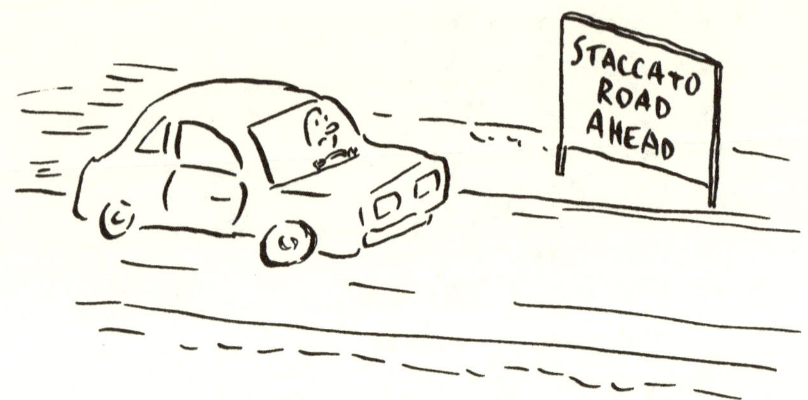
STACCATO
ROAD
AHEAD

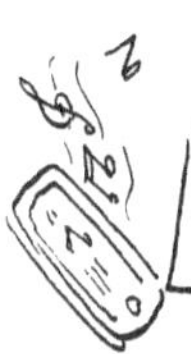

SUGGESTED RINGTONES

FOR YOUR EX 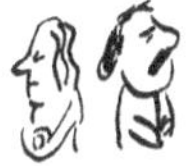 LA TRAVIATA

FOR YOUR BOSS 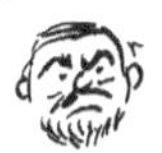 BORIS GODUNOV

FOR YOUR HEALTH INSURANCE COMPANY 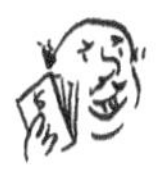 GOUNOD'S FUNERAL MARCH OF THE MARIONETTE

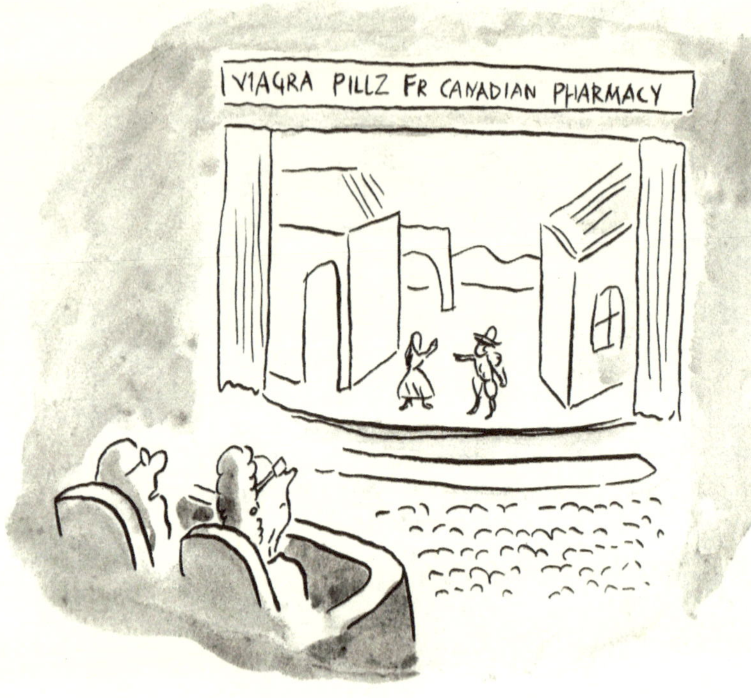

"Either they got a spam virus in the supertitles or this Don Giovanni production was desperate for sponsorship."

SYMPHONY #39
"THE ÜBER-COLOSSAL"

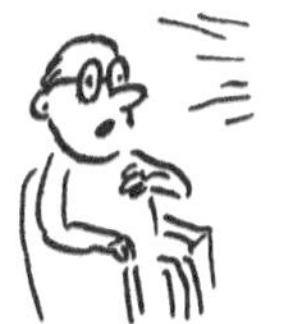

SYMPHONY #391
"THE OVER-THE-TOP"

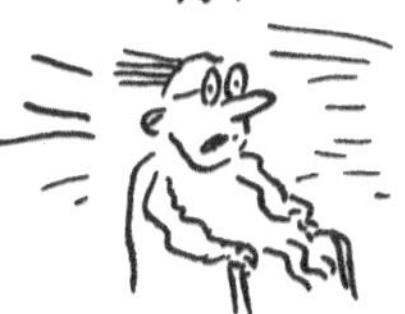

SYMPHONY #432
"THE CRIMINAL"

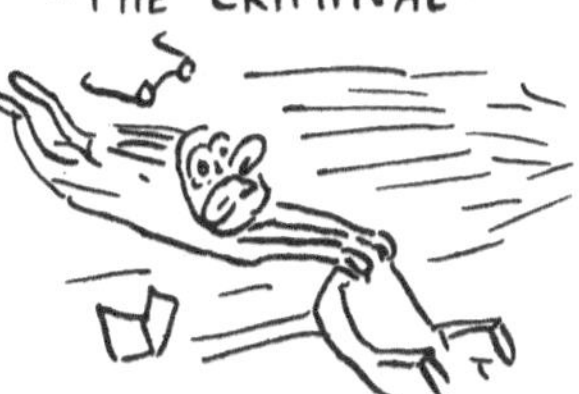

SYMPHONY #0
"THE PREPUBESCENT"

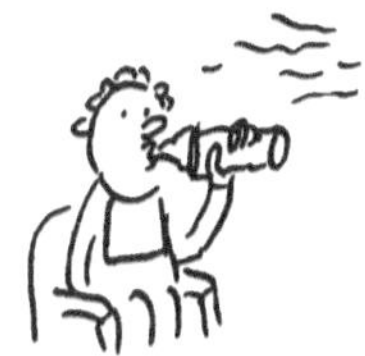

SYMPHONY #582
"THE ETERNAL"

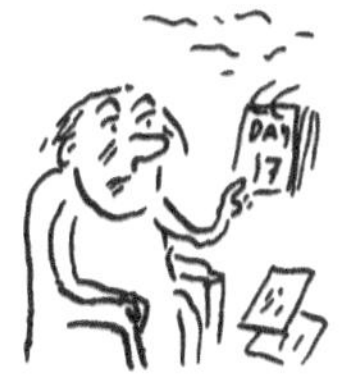

SYMPHONY #1342
"THE ESCAPE"

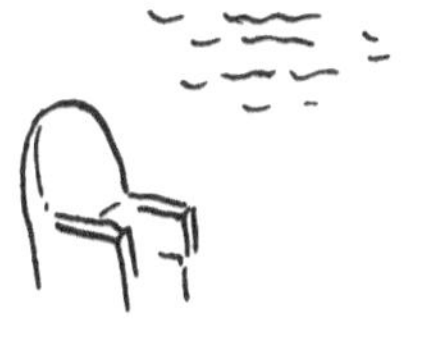

"I really hate it that you can't download Tartini's Devil's Trill Sonata around here."

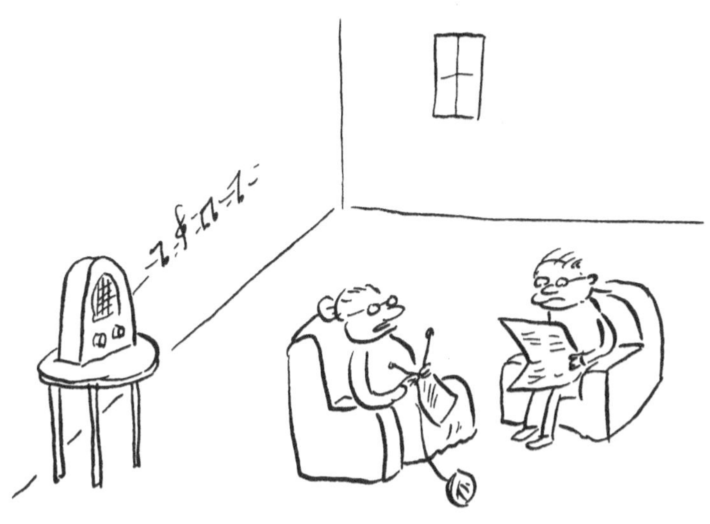

"That must be a recording – no one can play that well."

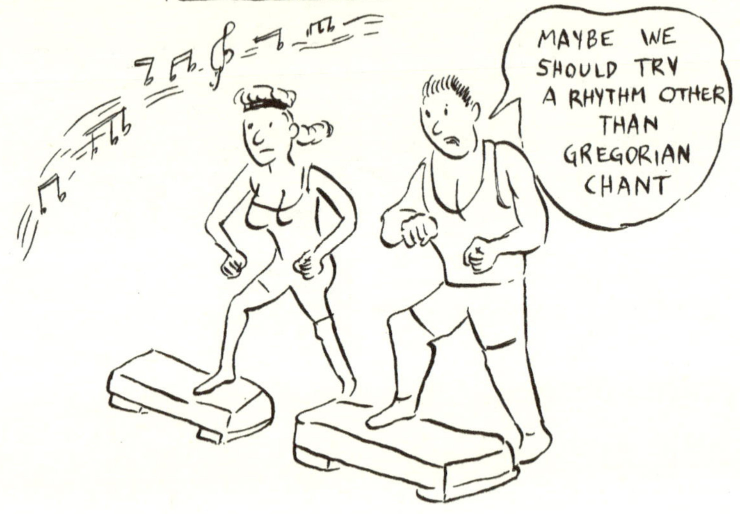
THE EARLY DAYS OF AEROBICS
MAYBE WE SHOULD TRY A RHYTHM OTHER THAN GREGORIAN CHANT

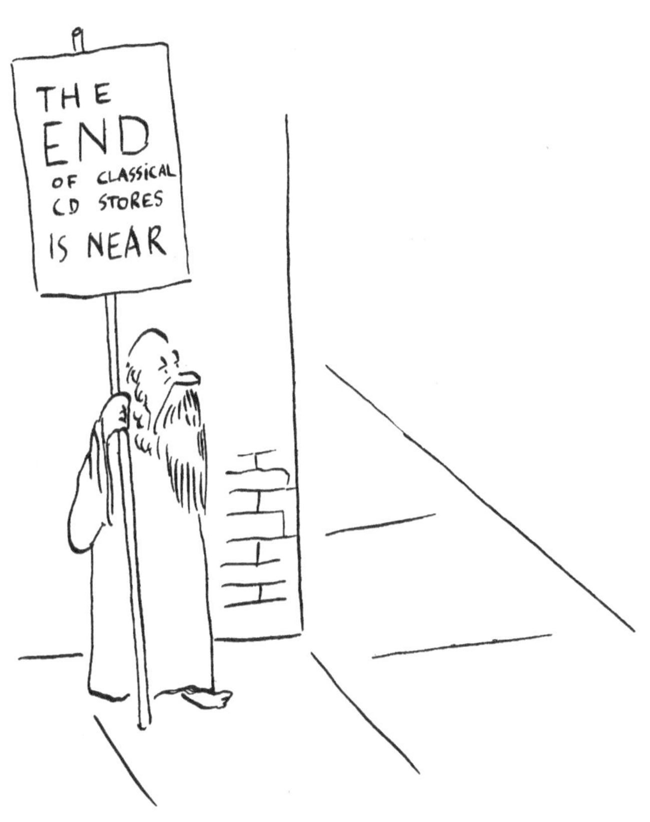
THE
END
OF CLASSICAL
CD STORES
IS NEAR

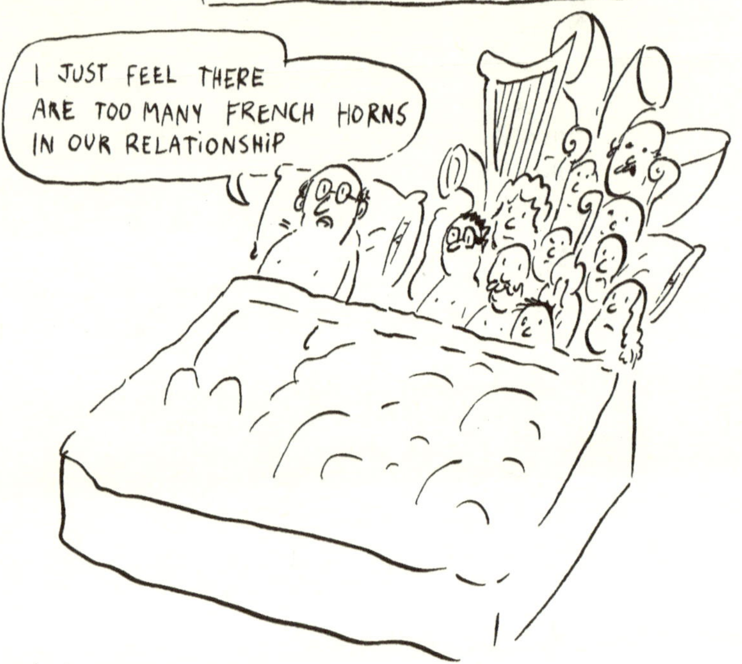
THE END OF THE (CONDUCTOR) AFFAIR
I JUST FEEL THERE ARE TOO MANY FRENCH HORNS IN OUR RELATIONSHIP

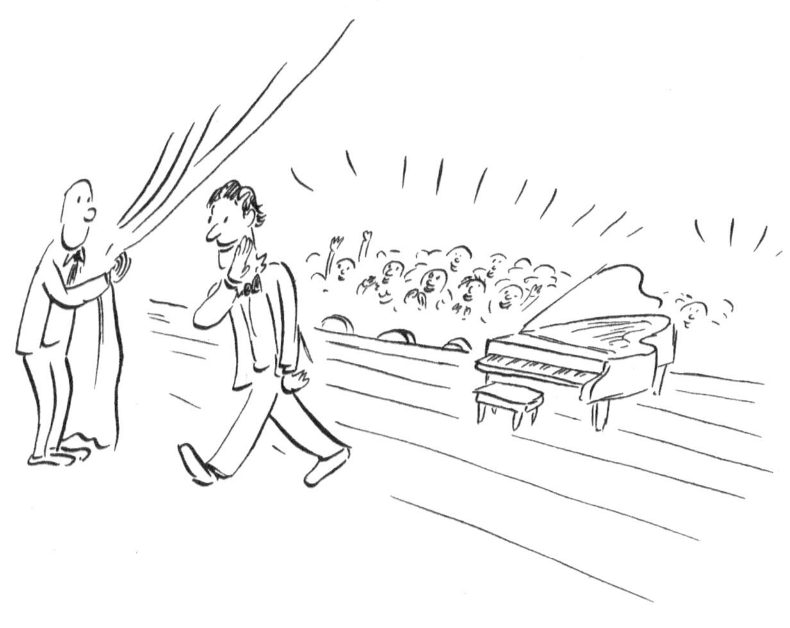

"The good thing about playing a virtually unknown contemporary piece is that no one realized I got lost for half an hour while in the middle."

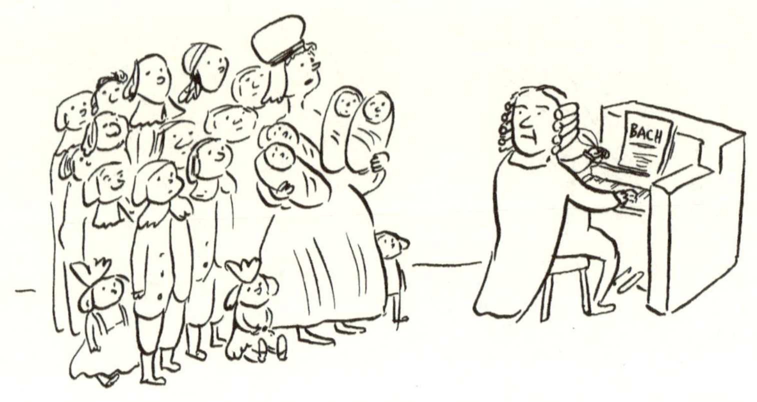

"The kids want to start a reality show."

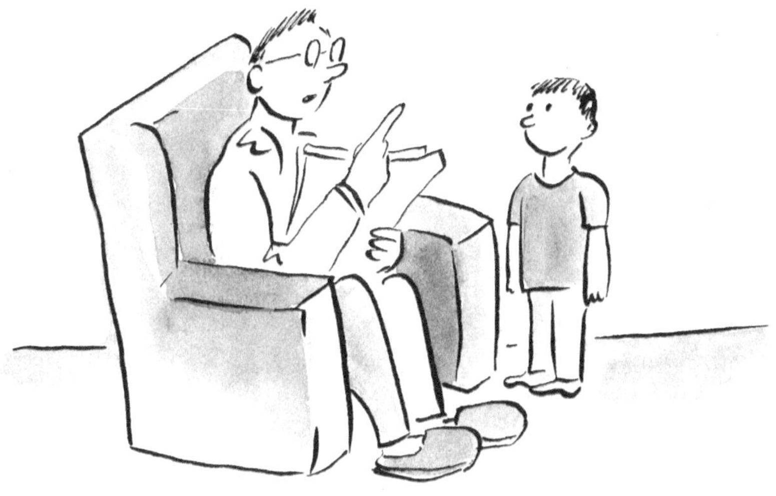

"Always remember: the only certainties in life are death, taxes, and clapping between movements."

MORE INNOVATIVE MUSIC GROUP NAMES

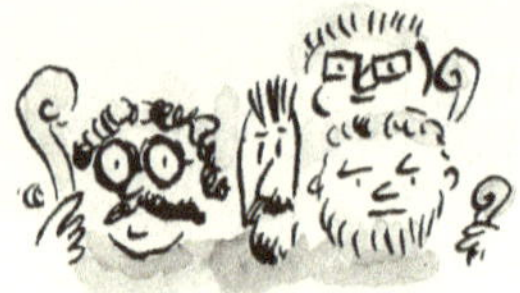

RIGATONI STRING QUARTET

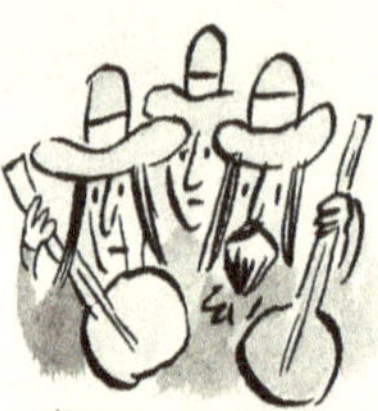

PALESTRINA BANJO ENSEMBLE

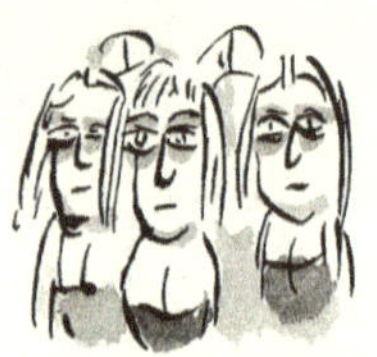

LADY GAGA MEDIEVAL CONSORT

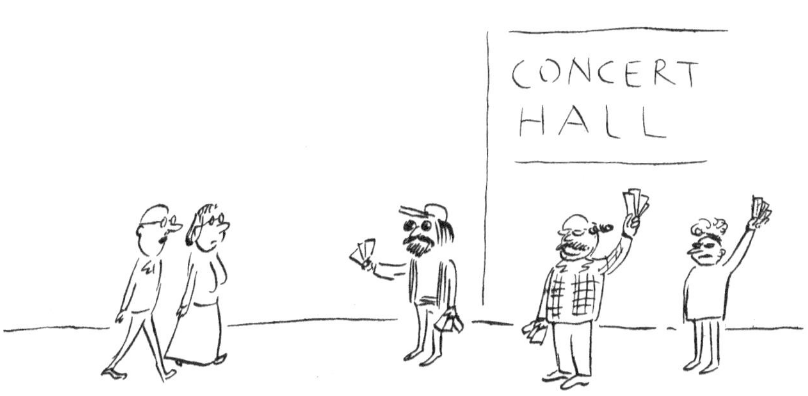

"I was hoping we would miss the scalper overture."

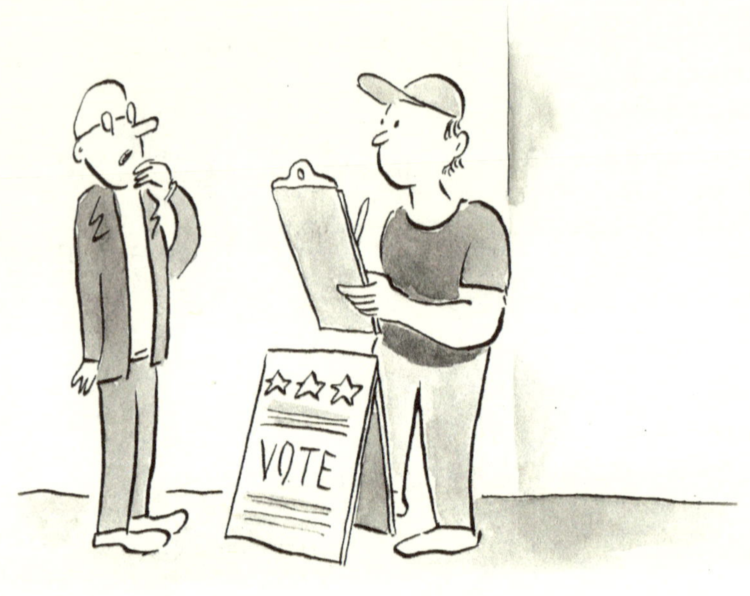

"Me? I consider myself more of a leaning Stravinsky moderate."

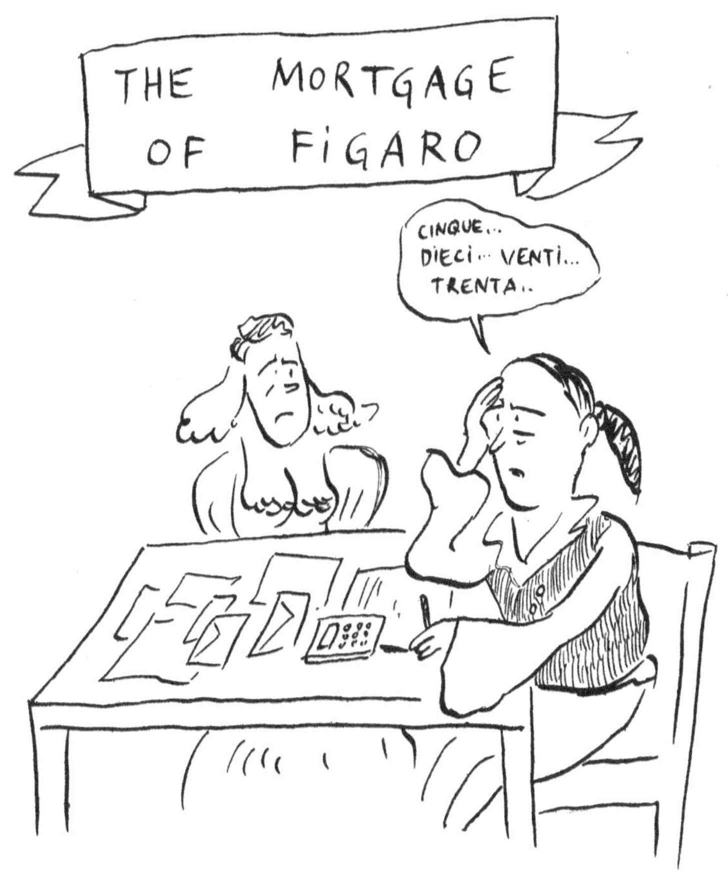
THE MORTGAGE OF FIGARO
CINQUE... DIECI... VENTI... TRENTA..

THE MUSIC PHARMACY

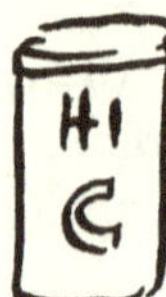

THE PERFECT VITAMIN TO REACH THAT TRICKY NOTE!

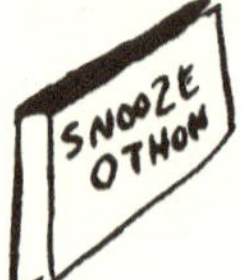

ONE PILL WILL LET YOU NAP THROUGH THE BORING MIDDLE PIECE IN THE CONCERT!

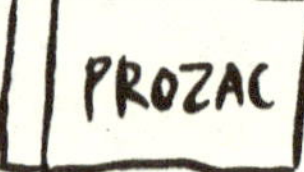

MAKES SCHUBERT SOUND LIKE SOUZA!

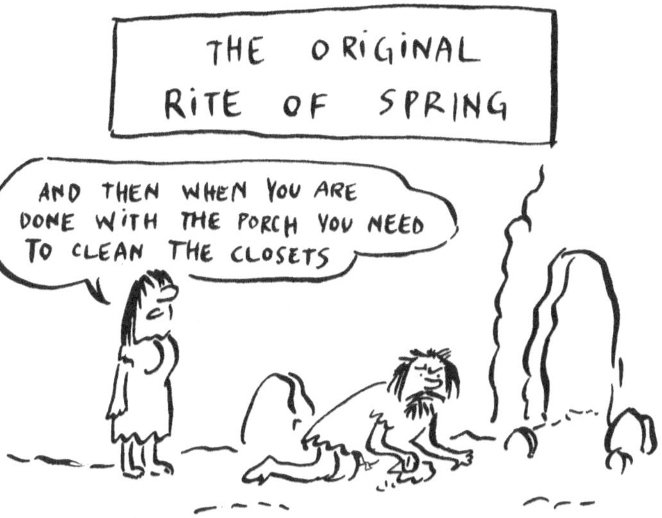

THE ORIGINAL RITE OF SPRING

AND THEN WHEN YOU ARE DONE WITH THE PORCH YOU NEED TO CLEAN THE CLOSETS

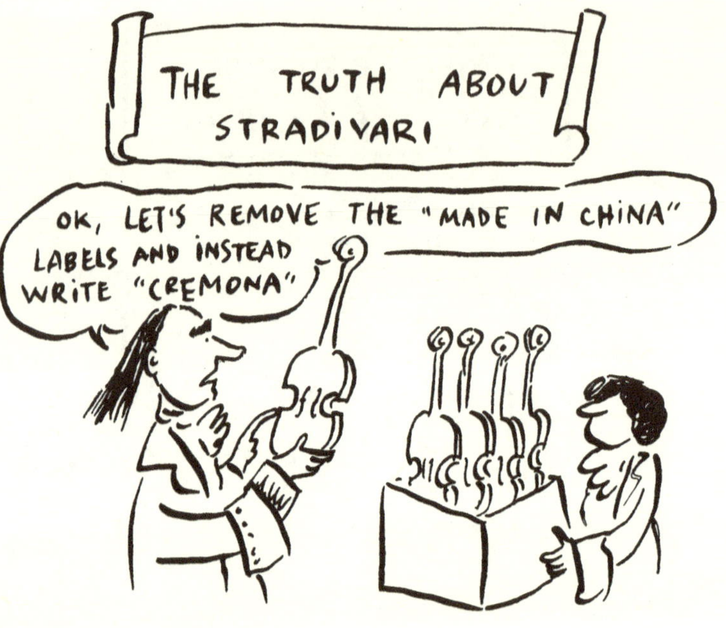
THE TRUTH ABOUT STRADIVARI
OK, LET'S REMOVE THE "MADE IN CHINA" LABELS AND INSTEAD WRITE "CREMONA"

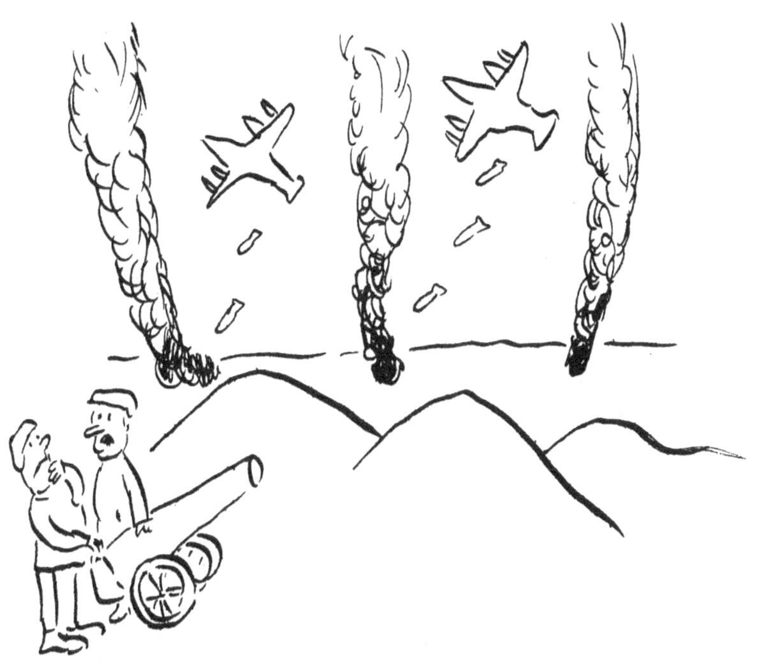

"The enemy may have smart bombs,
but they can't play the 1812 Overture."

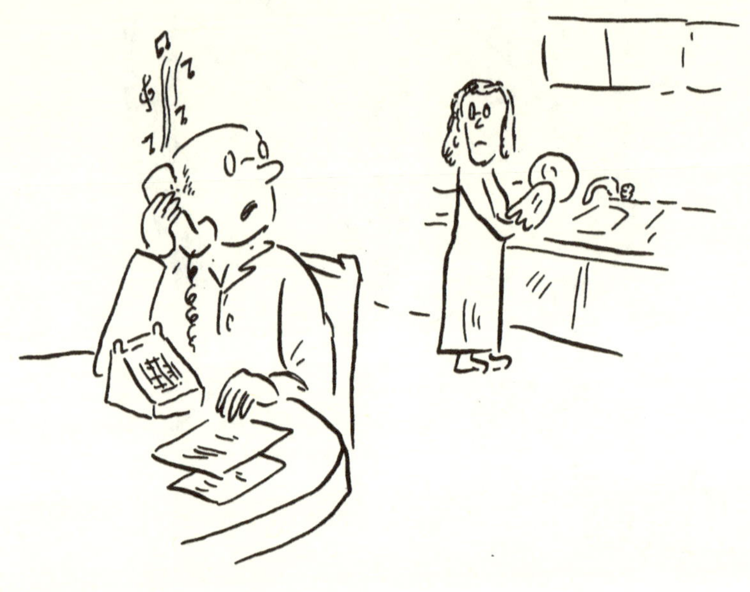

"This is not good – our mortgage lender put me on hold with the Danse Macabre on the background."

THUS SPAKE ZARATHUSTRA

SO AS I WAS SAYING...

SSHHH HONEY! LET'S KEEP YOUR MUSIC CRITICISM FOR AFTER THE CONCERT

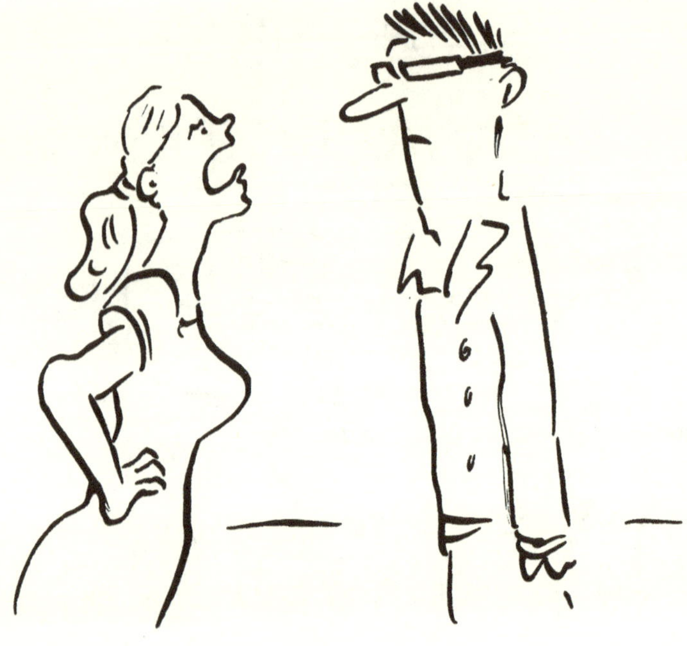

"You can't be both the tonic AND *the dominant of this relationship."*

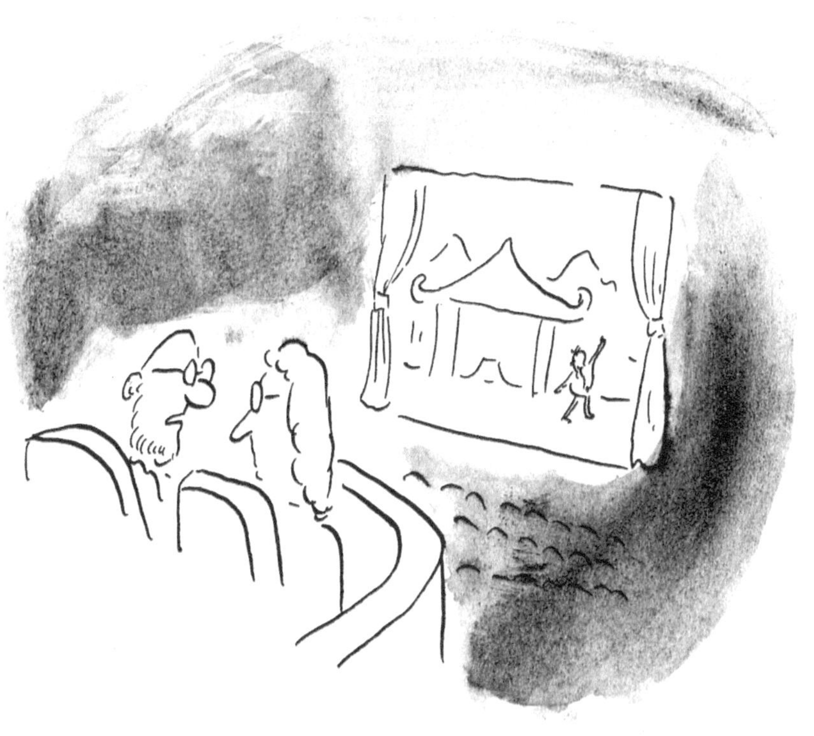

"In this production, Turandot has even less time to figure out Calaf's name because of Daylight Savings Time."

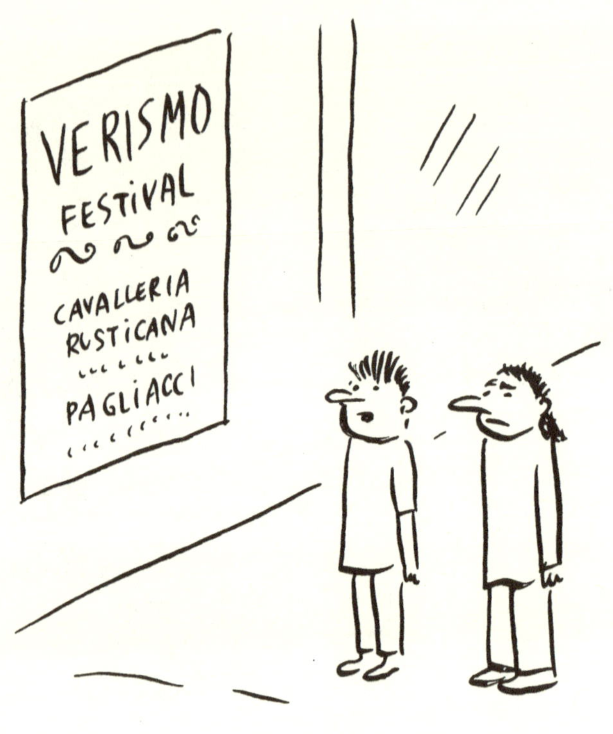

"It's like, what they had before reality TV."

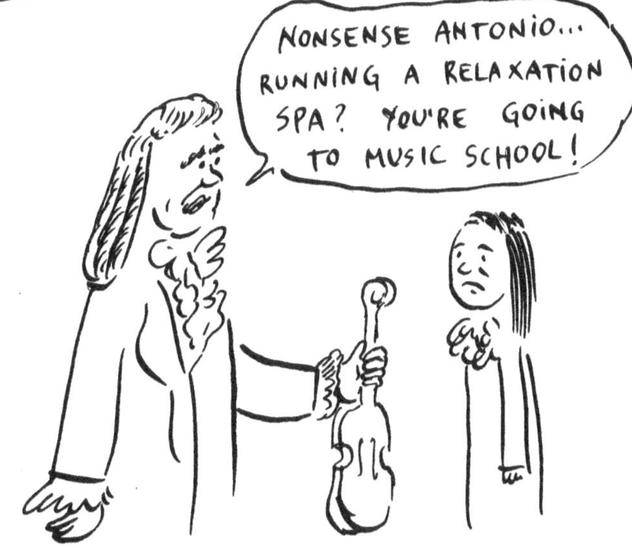
VIVALDI CHOOSES CAREERS
NONSENSE ANTONIO... RUNNING A RELAXATION SPA? YOU'RE GOING TO MUSIC SCHOOL!

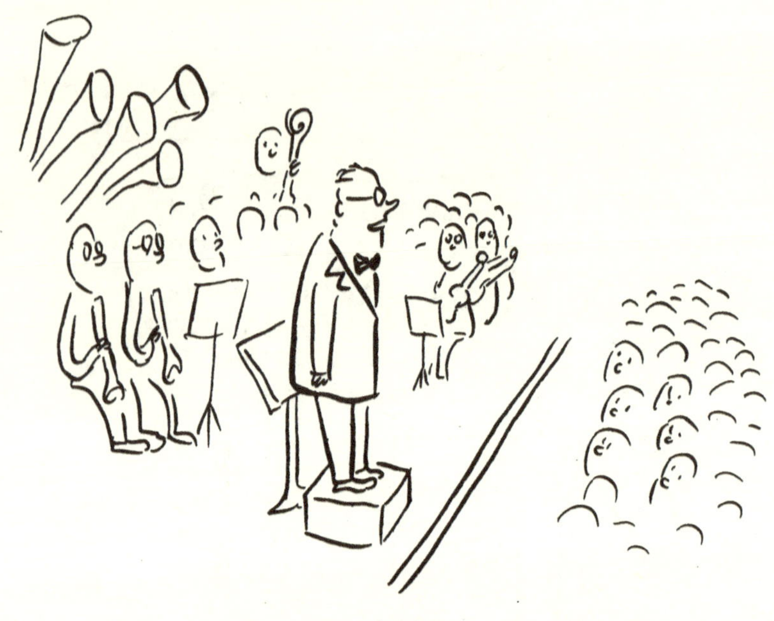

"Due to recent budgetary adjustments, the French Horn section has now been replaced by vuvuzelas."

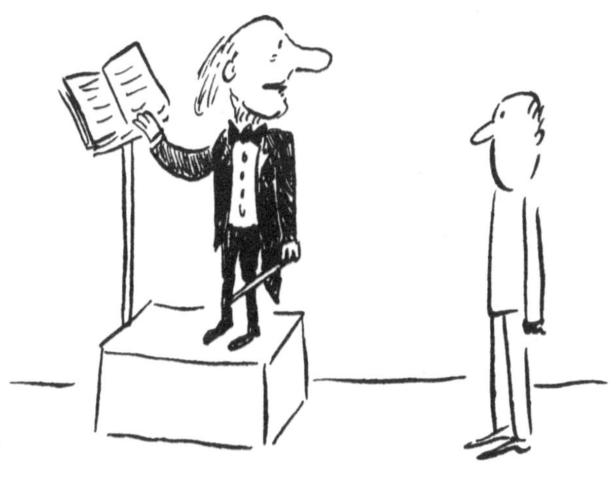

"We conductors live long because we suck the life out of the orchestra."

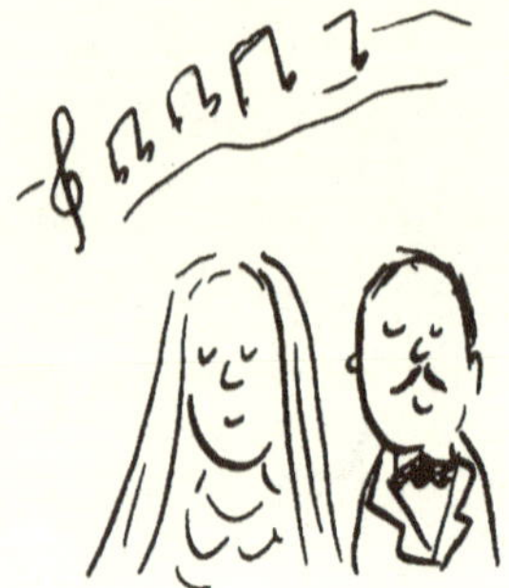

THE WEDDING MARCH

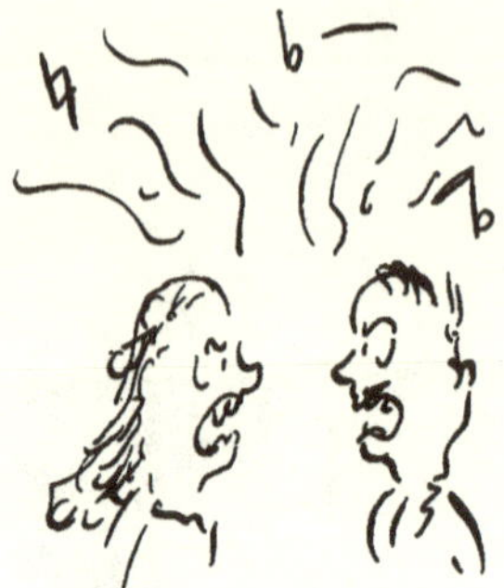

THE DIVORCE ORATORIO

The WELL-TEMPERED MOCHACCINO

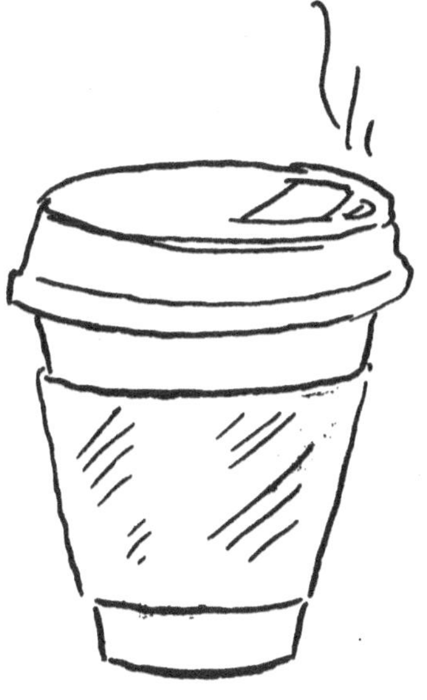

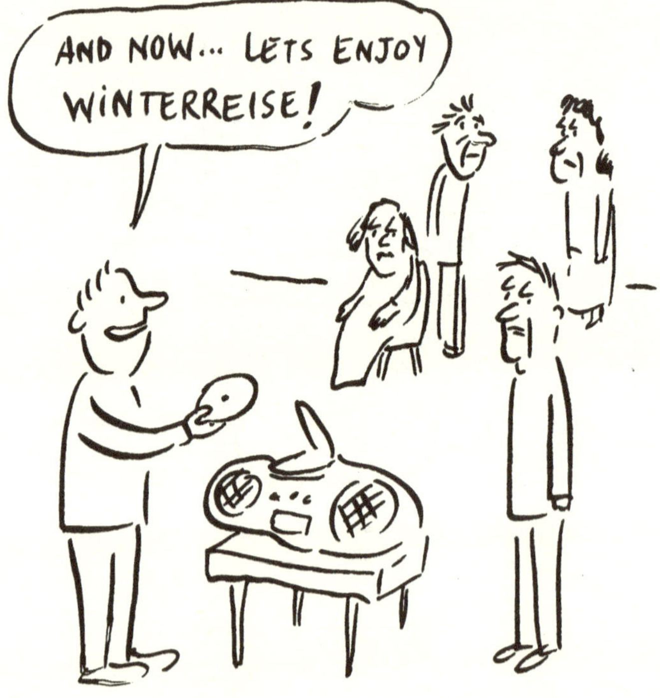
WHAT NOT TO PLAY TO A MANIC-DEPRESSIVE SUPPORT GROUP
AND NOW... LETS ENJOY WINTERREISE!

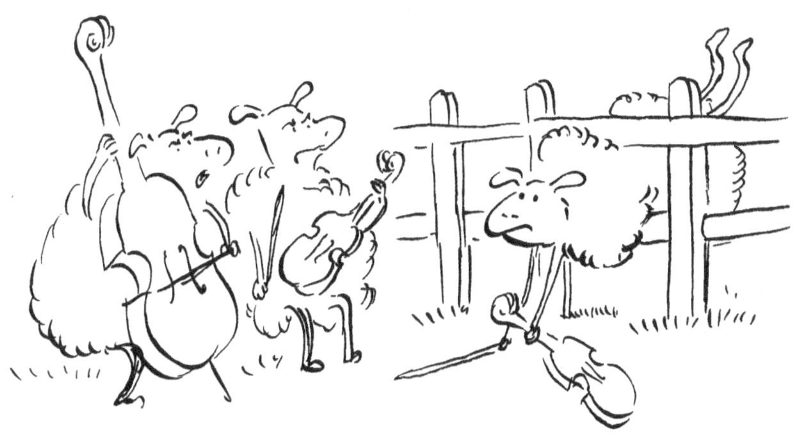

"You always get stuck on that passage!"

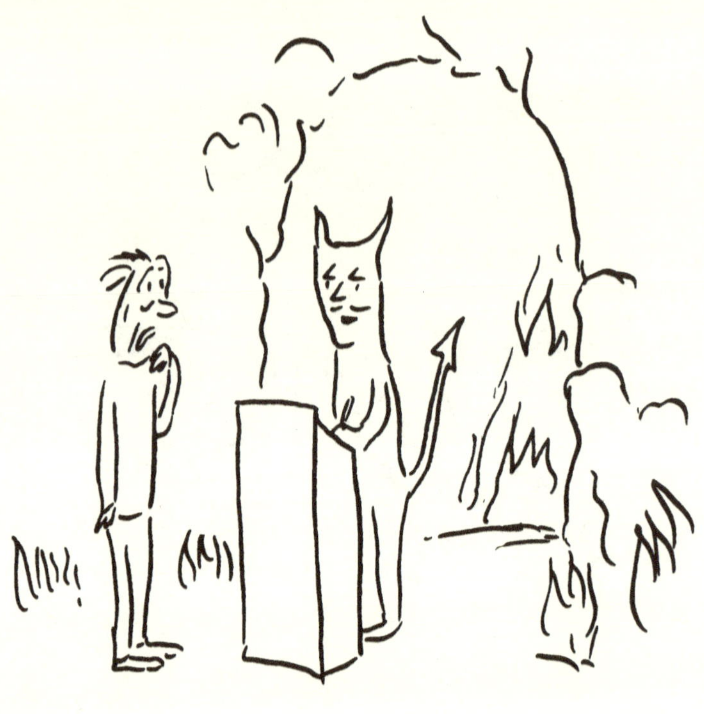

"You do get to choose your favorite Andrew Lloyd Weber musical for all eternity."

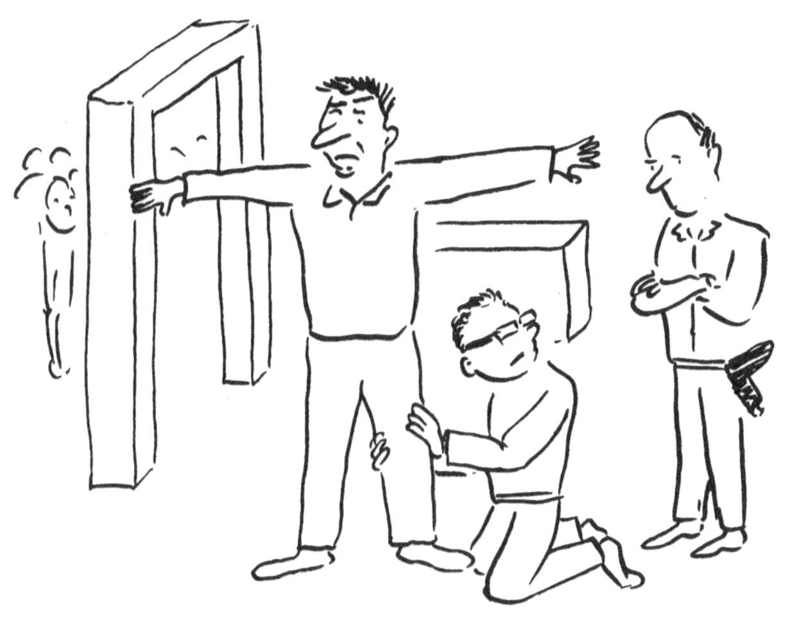

"You never know when your piano fingering techniques can come in handy."

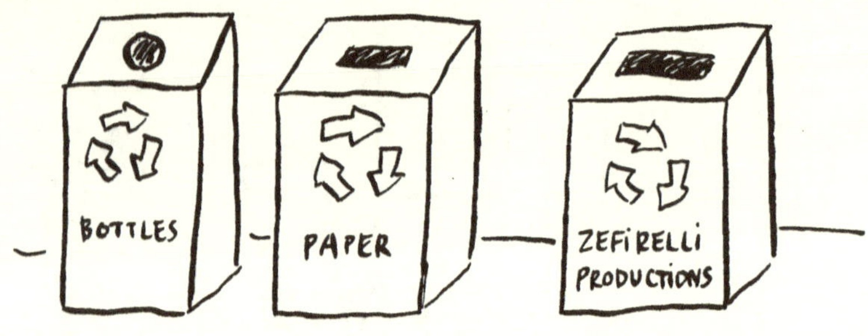
BOTTLES
PAPER
ZEFIRELLI PRODUCTIONS

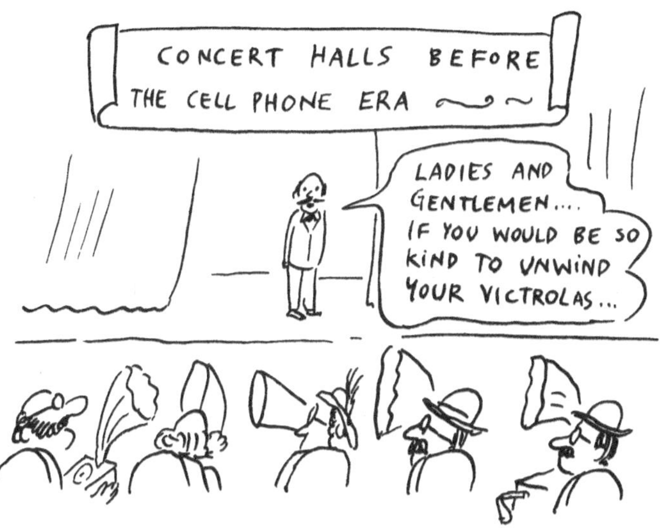
CONCERT HALLS BEFORE THE CELL PHONE ERA
LADIES AND GENTLEMEN.... IF YOU WOULD BE SO KIND TO UNWIND YOUR VICTROLAS...

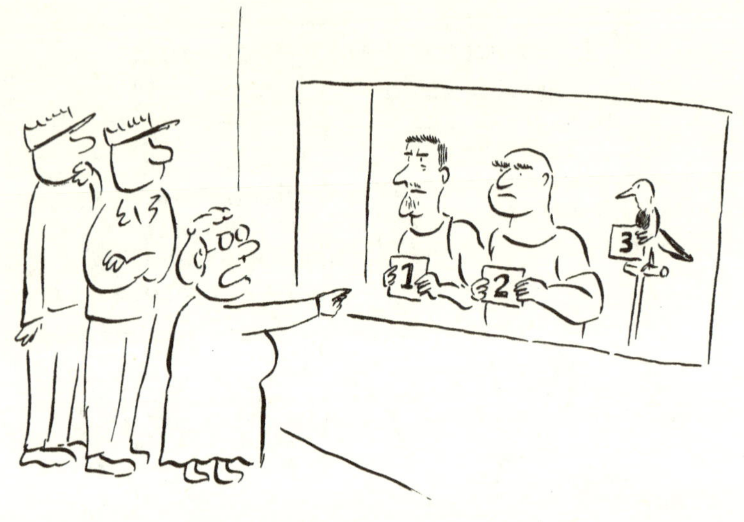

"That's the one! That's the thieving magpie."

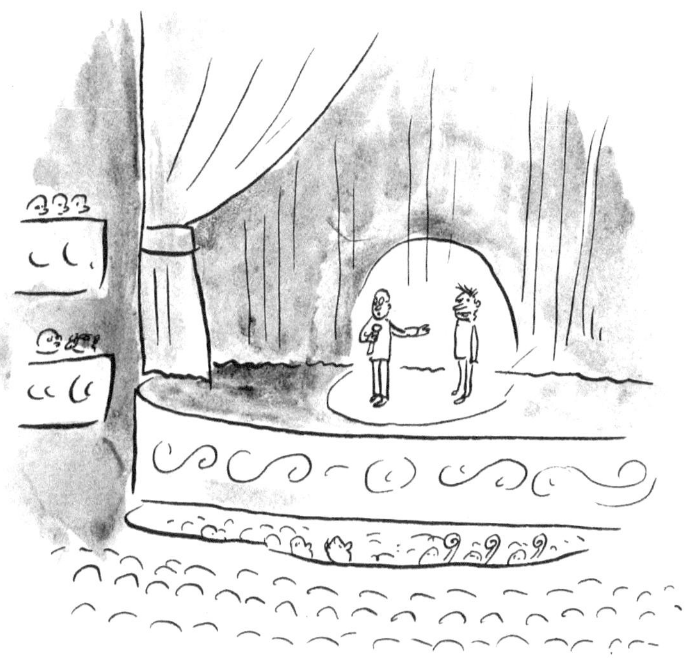

"The role of Siegfried will be interpreted tonight by this random guy we just grabbed from the street."

Tom Huizenga is a music producer, reporter and blogger for NPR Music. He hosts NPR's classical music blog *Deceptive Cadence* and contributes stories about classical music to NPR's news programs. He has produced live opera broadcasts from Washington's D.C.'s Kennedy Center, hosted string quartets at clubs in Manhattan and regularly invites artists to play and talk in the NPR performance studio.

Huizenga's radio career began at the University of Michigan, where he hosted jazz, opera and experimental radio programs at WCBN. As an Enthnomusicology student, he performed traditional court music from Indonesia, while also studying English Literature and voice. Before joining NPR, Huizenga served as music director for a NPR member station in New Mexico and taught radio production at New Mexico State University. He also writes about music for the *Washington Post.*

Pablo Helguera (born in Mexico City in 1971) is a visual and performance artist. Some of his past art projects have included a phonographic archive of dying languages, a memory theater, fourteen visual artist "heteronyms," and an exhibition about four fictional opera composers. In 2006 he drove from Anchorage to Tierra del Fuego with a collapsible schoolhouse, organizing discussions, activist happenings, and civic ceremonies along the way (*The School of Panamerican Unrest*). He has been the recipient of Creative Capital, Guggenheim, and Franklin Furnace fellowships, and in 2011 he was the first recipient of the International Award for Participatory Art, given by the Assembly of Emilia-Romagna, in Italy. He started publishing his cartoons in 1987 in the magazine *Pauta* in Mexico City. He is the author of three volumes of cartoons about the art world, known as *Artoons.* He is a regular cartoon contributor to The Art Newspaper and the NPR classical blog, *Deceptive Cadence.* His work has been exhibited widely in many biennials and modern and contemporary museums around the world.

Since 2007 Helguera has been Director of Adult and Academic Programs in the Department of Education at the Museum of Modern Art, New York. He is married to artist Dannielle Tegeder, and they live in Brooklyn with their daughter, Estela.

www.ingramcontent.com/pod-product-compliance
Lightning Source LLC
LaVergne TN
LVHW051012080826
845145LV00009B/2586

9781934978771